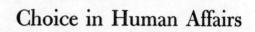

Choice in Human Affairs

HV3018.L93   ST. JOSEPH'S UNIVERSITY   STX
Choice in human affairs;

3 9353 00022 6876

Choice in Human Affairs

An Application to Aging-Accident-Illness Problems

ELMER LUCHTERHAND
Department of Sociology
Yale University

DANIEL SYDIAHA
Department of Psychology
University of Saskatchewan

with the assistance of
EDMOND LAPIERRE and ALEXANDER WINN

HV3018
.L93

82176

COLLEGE & UNIVERSITY PRESS · *Publishers*

NEW HAVEN, CONN.

Copyright © 1966 by
College and University Press Services, Inc.
All Rights Reserved

Library of Congress Catalog Card Number: 66-28601

MANUFACTURED IN THE UNITED STATES OF AMERICA BY
UNITED PRINTING SERVICES, INC.
NEW HAVEN, CONN.

TO OUR WIVES

PAT AND MARY JEAN

Foreword

If programs of guided social change are to succeed, more and more responsibility is going to have to be accorded the individuals in whom the change is desired. This deceptively simple proposition is sweeping through the "helping" professions and is challenging the "caretakers" in a total and dramatic way. Similarly, if programs of guided social change are to succeed, ingenuity must replace formalism in the design, conduct, and evaluation of the programs. Unfortunately, this second proposition is more honored in project grant requests than in actual field operations.

Together the two propositions help define the character of a particular kind of social action effort. Predicated on trust in and respect for the human beings involved, and, especially sensitive to the complex human attitudes and forms of behavior that characterize change situations, the "client-activist" kind of social action effort requires much that is new from change agents. It requires a willingness to take nothing as given, whether it be "common knowledge" evaluation of the components of jobs or of the industry-community relationship. It requires a willingness to train new candidates for previously nonexistent posts. It requires constructive attention to the oft-overlooked problems of transferring a change design to a new location. It requires sagacity and patience in helping a change design stay close to its original commitment and details, the temptation to stray being as great in projects as it is in human affairs. And, above all, the "client-activist" kind of social action effort requires a basic commitment to a particular mental health position: Men grow in strength and dignity only as they are ennobled by the challenges life sets them. Men are ennobled only as they are helped to claim and to resolve their own problems.

A growing number of existential situations are being transformed by new public and professional interest in "client-activist" matters. Expectant mothers are training to assist the delivering physician during their own "natural" childbirth. University students are pondering still better techniques of helping schools evaluate faculty and pass on tenure. Prison inmates have expanded their participation as novice teachers in prison school systems, even as indigenous community aides are being increasingly relied on by neighborhood clinics and schools. The federal anti-poverty program lends special impetus to the entire movement with its pledge of "maximum feasible participation." The poor are finally to have a say in the shaping of their own destinies, at least, that is, if the enabling legislation is taken at face.

Here, of course, is the rub of the matter. The enabling legislation cannot be taken at face value. Around the country the mayors have joined forces with the social welfare "establishment" and the staffs of many city poverty programs to help keep the poor in their place. Indigenous community aides run a serious risk of being co-opted and stunted, rather than aided, in their own personal growth. Inmates are checked by old-line wardens who have only illiberal state standards to meet. Students are blocked by administrators and teachers who perceive of them as meddlesome and pesky kids. And mothers-to-be who would experience birth in their own personal style are blocked by time-honored hospital practices that regard patients as helpless wards.

The struggle has been joined. And the ultimate outcome may be hinted at in the descriptive account that follows. Drs. Luchterhand and Sydiaha trace the development of a project to improve the placement of workers having physical impairments in plants of a major producer of aluminum ingot. The authors relate their project's origins to the feeling of many that no easy answers were available, but doing things the same old way would not do at all. The company's commonplace practice before the placement project was started—of routing handicapped employees to the janitorial service—cost all dearly. Change in the direction of consulting with employees and safeguarding their choice from among newly evaluated jobs struck the change agents as an exciting and promising alternative. The writers go on to relate the elaborate jockeying that is part of every change project, the considerable time that must pass before truth and fantasy are distinguishable, the prominence of key personalities, the rigors of evaluative analysis, and the intriguing theoretical gains available in every well-executed action project. The writers pay special attention to morale and motivation gains, the underdiscussed mental health components of industrial practices. Their properly qualified affirmation of the rewards possible from "client-activist" work has exciting implications far beyond the province of their case study.

If men are to surmount the temptation to give up, they must believe they have a fair chance to make a difference inside their own lives. Few challenges run as wide or as deep. The book that follows is a front-line report from the battle area, a skillful and useful account of an important gain in the real world for the philosophy of self-determination. It has much to teach us— as social scientists, as change agents, and, most especially, as human beings.

Department of Sociology   ARTHUR B. SHOSTAK
Wharton School
University of Pennsylvania
Philadelphia

Preface

The solving of social problems has rarely proceeded in orderly fashion. Witness the fact that we are now driving ahead on this continent and elsewhere with massive social programs in which only slight use is made of tested knowledge from the social sciences. The need to develop effective anti-poverty programs raises many questions of practical and theoretical importance. This book approaches some of these questions by describing a project for placing blue-collar workers who have experienced partial loss of physical capacity because of aging, accidents or illness. Presented in the form of a natural history and evaluation of the project, the book details the steps in the development of what came to be called a mutual system of placement.

The project, which was initiated a dozen years ago, classifies properly as a demonstration project, a term that has since come into use. The problem was defined, goals were specified, and a set of procedures developed to realize them. In one respect, however, the placement project hardly fits present-day notions of a proper demonstration. It began without fanfare, without special funds, and with a temporary staff of one. To sum it up, it was officially unimportant; not much was expected of it.

The mechanics of the mutual system of placement described here include analyses of the physical and environmental demands of jobs, and, in similar form, assessments of the physical capacities of employees. Besides making such detailed information conveniently available for placement purposes, the system helps workers through the crises of physical impairments by providing a choice of jobs.

Case studies are included to indicate some of the difficulties encountered. Interview material and data from company records show the impact of the system on life in a major unit of the Aluminum Company of Canada.

Developed as a means to enhance feelings of personal worth and competence in times of crisis in the employees' work lives, the notion of choice is advanced as a key concept for various kinds of preventive and therapeutic social programs. The case for broad application of this and other features of the mutual system of placement rests on the view that different social problems may be related by pervasive common elements. This view is a logical extension of the concept of social system as variously developed in the social sciences. The final chapter states:

> The characteristics of people classified as aging differ from those of young victims of accidents or illness. Yet all may experience some loss of autonomy and feelings of powerlessness. So too may the school dropout when he attempts to fill adult roles in an automating society, and so may the Negro confronting discrimination outside the ghetto wall. In all these different problem areas, there may be such common elements as loss of autonomy and feelings of powerlessness. A program that succeeds in one area may have something to offer for programs in another, if the success bears on common problem elements. We believe that many of the problems associated with inner-city neighborhoods of our great metropolitan areas have common elements for which the program concept of choice is a crucial one. It may well be that few, if any, program concepts have greater relevance for reducing this cluster of contemporary social problems.

The earlier reports about this program* introduced it to many people, most of whom were outside industry. After the first report, the Selective Placement Officer for the Arvida plants of the Company was invited to two White House conferences on the handicapped. Expressions of interest in the placement system came from the United States Department of Health, Education and Welfare; from the Canadian Department of Labour; from

---

* E. Lapierre, E. Luchterhand and J. Pilote, *The Arvida Placement System: Review of Initial Operation, June 1953–December 1956* (Montreal: The Aluminum Company of Canada, Ltd., 1957), mimeographed, 14 pages; Elmer Luchterhand, with the assistance of E. Lapierre and A. Winn, *The Mutual System of Placement* (Montreal: Staff Training and Research Division, Aluminum Company of Canada, Ltd., 1962), mimeographed, 66 pages.

a conference on aging in Connecticut; from state and provincial government units in the United States and Canada; from gerontological societies, community action agencies, labor unions, and from professional personnel organizations. It is hoped that this study will be helpful to all such groups, and that students will find in it a resource in the study of organization theory, industrial sociology, and social psychology.

Something should be said about the respective contributions of the authors. As director of the project in its beginnings, the first author carries primary responsibility for project planning and design, for previous reports on it, and for chapters one, two, three and seven, and for general editing of the present book.

The second author is primarily responsible for chapters four, five and six, which deal with evaluation of the project. Since no provision was made initially for evaluation of the project, he assumed responsibility for the development of evaluation criteria, and for the collection and analysis of data.

Acknowledgments

Much credit goes to the Staff Training and Research Division of the Aluminum Company of Canada, Montreal, for support and suggestions in preparing the early reports on the project, and the present book, and for initiating similar projects beyond Arvida Works. Many people who were in the head office of the Company at Montreal, or in plants at Arvida, Quebec, or Kitimat, British Columbia, deserve special thanks for their help. We mention particularly P. E. Bernard, Dr. Frank de N. Brent, L. P. Daigle, R. A. Fortier, J. J. Gagnon, Dr. H. O. L. Murray, Rodney Northey, R. E. Rosane and L. G. Tremblay. Particular credit goes to members of the original project committee at Arvida: Dr. Marc Lacerte, Fortunat Lafrance, Jacques Mailly, J. Alex. Morin and L. G. Mousseau. The help of Dr. J. A. Gaudet, who was also a member of the project committee, and of Dr. Gérard Michaud, both deceased, was invaluable. No single individual devoted more effort to the development of the project in day-to-day work than the first Selective Placement Officer at Arvida Works, Jules Pilote.

Special appreciation goes to the hourly-paid employees and their unions at Arvida Works and Kitimat Works of the Company. It will be clear from this study that the active cooperation and concurrence of the hourly paid in developing the procedures of the system determined its achievements. This is as it should be, for the hourly paid are the *raison d'être* of the placement system.

Our other debts are more difficult to list. The mutual system of placement stems from the contributions of many people. Various ideas have their origins in reports of the War Manpower Commission, Washington, D.C., prepared during World War II, and in works by Clark D. Bridges and Bert Hanman. Major credit for the work of the War Manpower Commission on selective placement must go to K. Vernon Banta, who was its principal employment specialist for persons with severe physical impairments. Banta pioneered in the development of selective placement procedures, using analyses of the physical demands of jobs.

Others whose ideas influenced the placement system are Dr. Howard A. Rusk, Dr. Donald P. Kent and the authors included in the bibliography. Dr. Maurice Schweizer introduced us to several important studies in the literature on rehabilitation, and Margaret Kleinfeld assisted with the bibliography. The list would be incomplete without mention of the helpful comments of students in classes taught by the authors at McGill University, Sarah Lawrence College and the University of Saskatchewan.

Special thanks are due to our secretaries. Mrs. Dorothy Taylor typed the first complete draft of the manuscript. Mrs. Erika Zabinski, with occasional help from Miss Jemma Plummer and Mrs. Muriel Carpenter, handled the revisions with great skill.

The President's Publication Fund, University of Saskatchewan, provided expenses of one of the authors for a trip to Arvida, Quebec, to gather data, and for part of the clerical work on the first draft. Mr. Robert Rauch helped with the technical preparation of the final manuscript.

Finally we wish to acknowledge the courtesy of the American Mutual Liability Insurance Company in permitting us to quote extensively in Appendix II from their publication, *Physical Abilities to Fit the Job* (Boston, 1956).

July, 1966

E. L. and D. S.

Contents

List of Tables

List of Tables—Continued

List of Figures

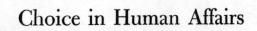

Choice in Human Affairs

1. The Problem and the Setting

The Problem of Placement

There are curious but important tendencies in societies to ignore or minimize their most serious social problems. Commenting on this, Kenneth Keniston writes:

> And most often they (the "troublesome characteristics") are taken for granted because their recognition would be painful to those concerned or disruptive to the society. Active awareness would at times involve confronting an embarrassing gap between social creed and social fact; at other times, the society chooses to ignore those of its qualities which subject its citizens to the greatest psychological strain.[1]

So it is that public provisions for treating poverty, disease and crime are typically inadequate to meet the needs of the society. To urge better treatment facilities would mean recognizing the gravity of the problems.

Many are the ways, conscious and unconscious, by which recognition is avoided. Instead of confronting the gap between creed and fact, it is common to pretend that there is none. A judge may send a man to prison, specifying that he should be given professional psychiatric treatment, even though provisions for such treatment are known to be nonexistent. Medical and social work professionals may do much toward the vocational rehabilitation of accident or illness victims, while ignoring the utterly inadequate provisions to re-employ persons whose physi-

[1] Kenneth Keniston, "Social Change and Youth in America," in E. H. Erikson (ed.), *Youth: Change and Challenge* (New York: Basic Books, Inc., 1964), p. 161.

cal capacity is impaired in any way. Or, workers with generally reduced capacities may be re-employed on janitors' jobs that are physically demanding, because of a curious willingness to credit a work-world myth that they are light-work jobs.

Side-stepping social problems is a deeply cultural matter. In a society that glorifies youth, who worries about the aging? In an urban industrial order that values speed and dexterity, who concerns himself with the disabled? Where everyone is seeking status, who is interested in janitors?

Somehow people and circumstances arise to prevent trouble-some social issues from being "swept under the rug." The honor roll of those who have helped to bring such issues to conscious-ness and conscience is long and brilliant. The list of contributing circumstances is also long. Thus World War II, with its material demands on the rear and its casualties at the front, posed sharply the need to cope with physical impairments through rehabilita-tion and placement. The military selected the best physical specimens. Industry, which had become enamored with the new personnel gadgetry for "selecting the best," suddenly found itself hiring anybody it could get. With public pressure to set new records in quantity and quality of production, attention in per-sonnel practice shifted somewhat from selection to placement.

At the war's end, there were the needs of disabled veterans for aftercare and employment. The Korean War, military inter-vention in Vietnam, and traffic accidents have added vast num-bers of disabled. Those with work records turn to past em-ployers; the very young enter the labor market as new goods marked "seconds." For industry the disabled are counted as so many placement problems; for the anti-poverty campaigns they comprise a special program population.

Recent developments in the factory system are adding greatly to placement problems and to public consciousness of them. In the community of artisans of other generations, aging workers tended to have more standing, authority and security than did most young workers. Until fairly recently, the craft hierarchy in industry tended to sustain this position of the aging skilled worker to the end of his work career. The breakdown of the craft hierarchy in recent times has had important effects on the worker's outlook and life chances.[2] In particular, the relationship between age and social position in the blue-collar world has been largely disrupted by changes in production methods. While the introduction of assembly-line techniques changed the skill requirements of many jobs, the industrial revolution known as automation is utterly transforming them. Trades of long and honorable standing in the blue-collar world are being disestablished. While many new jobs require very high skills, few call for the range of skills which the craftsman had to display.

For many employees the present transformations in production technology are highly disturbing. There are no longer the well-marked routes to mastery of a finite number of established trades. In their stead are unknown numbers of new skills which are not only poorly defined but changing. In effect, many employees are barred from progressing with age to positions of higher pay and prestige. For them the new changes in the factory system mean a relative loss of position; for others the loss is absolute. David Riesman has remarked the effect on factory life of shifting older workers to low-status jobs like elevator man or sweeper: "these men cast their shadows before, and make the plant itself seem a graveyard of hope and energy."[3]

Along with the widespread tendency for the status of older workers to be reduced, goes a similar one for persons with impairments caused by accidents or illness. As noted already, these tendencies have cultural dimensions as well as new technological ones. The general prospect is one of problems which are difficult to solve. In the next section we view them in a particular industrial context.

Plant and Community

How do the general problems of aging, accident and illness look in a particular plant and community? The Aluminum Company of Canada has its largest smelter, as well as other production units and a laboratory, at Arvida, Quebec. On the average

[2] W. L. Warner and J. O. Low, *The Social System of the Modern Factory* (New Haven: Yale University Press, 1947), chapters IV and V.

[3] David Riesman in his introduction to Ely Chinoy, *Automobile Workers and the American Dream* (New York: Doubleday, 1955), p. xvi.

there are some 5,000 hourly paid employees at this location. In 1954 when work was begun on developing a better placement system, the company faced a considerable accumulation of unsolved placement problems. The extent of the problem of aging can be seen in Table 1, which shows the number and the mean age of the hourly paid employees at Arvida Works. The four calendar dates listed were chosen because they represent immediately the employment peak for the year. In the eight years covered by this table, the number of hourly paid workers was reduced by about 3,000, largely because of curtailment of production. The increase in mean age for the eight years from 1955 to 1963 is 7.91 years, or nearly a year per year. This indicates that, under seniority rules, the reduction in the size of the work force affected the workers in the younger age categories more than those in the older ones.

From Table 1 it is clear that the aging of the Arvida work force follows the trend of the general population. Never before has there been such a high proportion of persons in the population who are over 50. "Never before was being 'old' so certain a prospect for so many."[4] Long life for large numbers is a general achievement of our urban industrial civilization, and the particular achievement of medical science. But for many aging people, adding years may not seem to be an achievement, but only the prolongation of despair. It is one thing to add years to life, but quite another to add life to those years—to make it possible to fill meaningful social roles. This is a task for general social planning and specifically for better placement procedures in the world of work.

TABLE 1. *Mean Age of the Hourly Paid at Arvida Works on Selected Dates, 1955-63, at the Seasonal Peak in Employment*

Date	Mean Age	No. of Hourly Paid
1963 (May 1)	44.30	4,459
1960 (April 28)	40.67	5,505
1958 (May 13)	39.01	5,454
1955 (April 4)	36.39	7,479

[4] Clark Tibbits and Wilma Donahue (eds.), *Aging in Today's Society* (Englewood Cliffs, New Jersey: Prentice-Hall, 1960), p. xvii.

Besides an aging work force, another important factor is that Arvida is basically a one-industry town. A city of 14,000, it was planned by the Aluminum Company of Canada and named after one of the industry's founders. Construction began in 1925, guided by a master plan. Originally the homes were company owned, but almost all were sold to employees more than ten years ago. Many others have been built by the city's residents since World War II.

Arvida Works is the world's largest industrial unit for producing primary aluminum. It employs the overwhelming majority of the town's male workers along with some women in the offices and laboratories. In addition to the aluminum plant, there is a small abrasive manufacturing plant and a smaller cement mixing plant. There are also construction firms, a machine repair shop, and a bakery. To all intents and purposes, however, Arvida is a one-industry town. How this fact underscores the need for improved selective placement will now be indicated.

Within a ten-mile radius of the plant (see Figure 1) live nearly 100,000 French Canadians, most of whom are concentrated in five cities: Arvida, Chicoutimi, Chicoutimi-Nord, Jonquière and Kenogami. Within the twenty-mile radius indicated by the broken line in Figure 1 live another 25,000.

How does this population outside Arvida affect employment practices? To answer this, Table 2 presents the ratios of average hires per month to applications in force from different locations in the employment recruiting area for Arvida Works.

The dates chosen precede the formal inauguration of a new system for placing employees having physical impairments. In each year, the ratio of average hires per month to applications in force was significantly higher for the city of Arvida than for the other areas indicated. The data leave no doubt that a higher proportion of Arvida job applicants are hired than others. It would be surprising if this were not the case, both because of the operation of community sentiment and because of concern with community relations. Whatever the relevant weight of these factors, it seems clear that to be highly selective toward local applicants would place a great many important relationships in jeopardy.

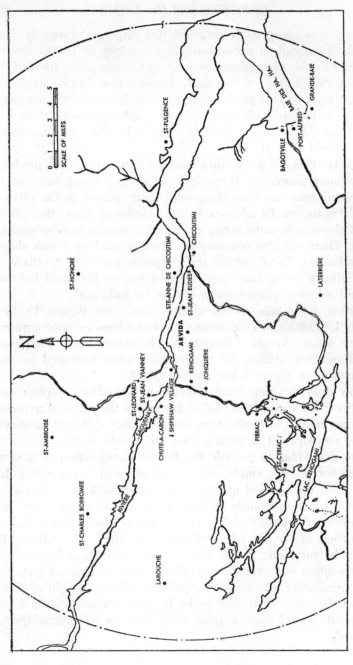

FIGURE 1. Arvida and the Employee Recruiting Area

TABLE 2. *Ratio of Hires to Applications in Force, by Location of Residence, 1954 and 1955*

RATIO OF HIRES TO APPLICATIONS IN FORCE

| | Location of Residence | | | Other Locations within 20-mile radius |
Year	Arvida	Jonquière-Kenogami	Chicoutimi	
1954	.173	.053	.048	.095
1955	.282	.063	.051	.034

The Nature of the Industry

One of the compelling reasons for better selective placement is the nature of the industry. There are three basic industrial processes involved in the production of aluminum: extraction, reduction, and casting and alloy production. As is the case with other forms of heavy industry, these processes expose employees to noxious environments.

The first of the three industrial processes is the extraction of aluminum oxide (alumina) from bauxite. It is carried out in two plants adjacent to the smelting and fabricating plant. The second process is the reduction of alumina to aluminum, and is achieved in an electrolytic cell called a "pot." Electric power is fed to these pots or reduction cells in groups of about 130 in series. Such a group of pots operating on one electric circuit is called a "pot line." Molten aluminum is drawn from the pots at intervals and transported to holding furnaces in which it is prepared for casting into ingots. This third industrial process includes the production of alloys by adding iron, copper, magnesium, manganese, titanium or other alloying elements. Most of the metal is shipped in ingot form for fabrication elsewhere, but a substantial amount goes to a rod rolling mill within the plant.

The various industrial processes have been outlined here (and are described in some detail in Appendix I) to indicate the nature of the work environment as one contributor to employee disabilities. As in all heavy industry, large numbers of complex machines are a factor in accidents. Chemical processes involve some exposure to noxious vapors. Furnaces, rotary kilns, and pot lines mean exposure to high temperatures. Despite recent substantial improvements, smoke and dust continue to be a problem in the pot rooms. Although efforts to reduce these noxious elements in the work environment are continuous, major achievements occur slowly and at great cost.

Developments in Vocational Rehabilitation

In many industries, including aluminum smelting and fabricating, specialization and subdivision of jobs has in the last decades increased the possibility of placing productively employees having reduced physical capacity due to aging, accident or illness. One important element in the situation is the fact that ways have been developed to overcome the handicapping effects of impairments. Advances in therapy, training, and other aids to adjustment have been considerable. Medical knowledge in the use of new drugs, in surgical procedures, and in means for assessing progress of therapy has increased greatly. Also substantial gains have been made in the development of specialized rehabilitation centers where the multiple problems of disabled persons are brought to the attention of members of various professions. The various therapies employed have increasingly been concerned with the whole man. Finally, in regard to prosthetic aids, decided advances have been made. Artificial limbs are now lighter and more reliable and more nearly simulate the functions of lost members. Training in the use of prosthetic appliances has similarly progressed. Advances in electronic hearing aids and procedures for testing and fitting them are well known.

Another important development is the changing concept of disability. In some companies, employment interviewers and placement people still look for the "perfect anatomical specimen." They seem to be unaware of how far this view lags behind approaches of modern medicine. It is meaningless to think of competence in terms of anatomical perfection. The notion of disability itself is similarly undergoing revision. When a disability no longer disables a person occupationally, it need not be thought of as a disability. For a worker with a physical impairment that obliges him to change his occupation, the real meaning of disability is a more or less severe limitation on his job choices. When he has been well placed and has made a satisfactory adjustment, limitation on choice ceases to be a problem. Occupationally, he is no longer any more disabled than other employees who have made a similar adjustment, but without apparent physical limitation on their choices.

Janitor Jobs and Placement

Among workers, each job is ranked in several ways. It is tagged as easy or hard, clean or dirty, safe or dangerous. The difficulty, dirt, or danger may largely belong to company history. The tags tend to change with the facts, but the fit is never perfect. Each job is also placed somewhere on a general scale of good-to-poor. What "good" means is often unclear, since it refers to a combination of qualities. "Good" may point chiefly to pay, working conditions or other factors. How jobs are defined often depends greatly on who the incumbents are: A job may be "good" because the incumbents rank high in the opinion of their fellows —the "best guys" work on it. That it takes a good man to handle a good job is a blue-collar claim to status—one which can lead placement officers to some wrong conclusions. Thus, it is commonly assumed that "most anyone" can do janitor work, because it is a poor job. This explains the tendency to view the janitor job as the solution to the placement of aging, accident and illness cases.

In analyzing the physical demands of jobs at Arvida Works (discussed below) to develop better selective placement, it became clear that janitor jobs were, in most instances, nearly as demanding physically as the run of jobs in the Works. In view of this, it is of some interest to look at the basis on which the members of the janitor service were assigned to it before 1954 when work was begun on developing a better placement system.

From Table 3 it may be seen that as of April, 1954, 89 per cent of the janitors at Arvida Works had been assigned to their jobs because of physical impairments or aging. Implicit in this situa-

TABLE 3. *Reasons for Assignment to the Janitor Service of All Janitors at Arvida Works in April 1954*[*]

TRANSFERRED FROM OTHER DEPARTMENTS

| | Total | Physically Impaired | | Physi- cally unable to do previous job | Over 50 years old | No reason given | Engaged as Janitors |
		by acci- dent	by ill- ness				
Number of Employees	155	20	55	16	47	10	7
Per cent	100	13	36	10	30	6	5

[*] These data are taken from a company memorandum, Arvida Works, March 30, 1954.

tion was the use of the janitor service by placement people as a catchall for those regarded as physically unfit. What the table does not show, and what could not be known in 1954, was that many of the men in the service could have been productively employed elsewhere in Arvida Works. Instead they were concentrated in the janitor service, with injury to their self-esteem and, in turn, to the service. Finally, the service deteriorated until it became an object of study by the industrial engineers at the request of the Assistant Works manager.

From Table 4 it may be seen that, as of April, 1954, the age distribution of the janitors was heavily skewed toward the upper brackets. Sixty-eight per cent were 50 or more years old, and only 6 per cent were under 40.

How did the placement practices summarized in Tables 3 and

TABLE 4. *Age Distribution of Janitors at Arvida Works in April 1954*[*]

	Total	20-29 years	30-39 years	40-49 years	50-59 years	Over 60 years
Number of Employees	155	3	6	40	75	31
Per cent	100	2	4	26	48	20

[*] These data are taken from a company memorandum, Arvida Works, March 30, 1954.

4 affect general employee attitudes? Alcan studies in other plants suggest that the influence of such practices was negative, but no Arvida evidence on this point can be offered here. It may be mentioned, however, that the janitors are rather evenly distributed throughout the Works, have daily contact with a great many employees, and informally gather and pass along many bits of news and gossip. It is logical to suppose that, in the phrase by Riesman quoted earlier, they "cast their shadows before. . . ." The data on length of service of the janitors made this all the more likely. Table 5 shows that of the 155 janitors in April, 1954, 118 or 76 per cent had ten or more years of service with the company.

TABLE 5. *Length of Service of Janitors at Arvida Works in April 1954**

	Total	Under 5 years	5-9 years	10-14 years	15-19 years	Over 20 years
Number of Employees	155	11	26	67	30	21
Per cent	100	7	17	43	19	14

* These data are taken from a company memorandum, Arvida Works, March 30, 1954.

Prospects

While our main interest at this point is with Arvida Works, it is only fair to point out that the pattern which existed there through 1954, as indicated by Tables 3, 4 and 5, is still prevalent in modern industry. Is there some compelling logic behind this pattern? Our answer is "no." Logic has little or nothing to do with this, but only work-world myths and placement habits. Although the janitor job is generally a "poor" one by pay and other standards, it is one which rational planning can usually make better.

The important point here is that wherever job evaluation is based on multiple factors, physical demands of jobs tend to be of slight importance in determining rates of pay. Pay and physical demands may even be negatively correlated—low pay may go with generally high physical demands. This pattern has obvious importance in designing and developing placement procedures for employees with physical impairments due to aging, accidents or illness.

In the next chapter we describe a project which involved a careful and detailed reappraisal of placement practices. We will describe how a project committee came into being and went about its work. The chapter points out how physical disabilities were treated as everyone's problem ultimately and how hourly-paid employees of all ages and departments were involved in the development of new placement procedures.

2. The Project: Selective Placement by Choice and Consent

Individual concern with selective placement arises out of human needs and sympathy. As noted already, the factors behind public concern with selective placement may be quite complex. Among those mentioned were wars, changes in the factory system, the achievements of medicine, and particular features of plant and community subcultures. The question arises as to how individual and public concern may be turned into planful action.

The importance of good committee work in designing and effecting social programs can hardly be overstated. When it is slighted in the planning and design phase, programs may be malformed; when it is neglected during the operating phase, they may die. In this chapter we look closely at the project committee which developed the mutual system of placement evaluated in this study.

In September, 1954, the Staff Training and Research Division of the Aluminum Company of Canada, Montreal (Alcan) loaned one of its research associates[1] to Arvida Works for a period of in-plant training. There the researcher was offered a choice of plant problems "to solve." One of the most besetting of these was the growing accumulation of unmet placement needs of employees with physical impairments.

The exploratory work on this problem took the form of talks with various people working in safety, first aid and health, employment, industrial relations, and production. There were also several discussions with the personnel manager. No one had a clear answer to the question of how to take care of the immediate placement needs, or how to prevent future accumulations. Everyone seemed agreed that the problem merited serious concern. Some felt it had arisen because the employment office failed

---

[1] The first author.

to select the best physical specimens, and that future accumulations could be avoided by setting stricter employment standards. Others felt that it was necessary to increase the number of early retirements as much as possible. The "successes" of other companies in Canada and the United States in reducing the age of their work forces by this means were cited. Some felt that steps should be taken to bring in more light industry, such as a subsidiary producer of aluminum goods. Several people said, that whatever kind of program was undertaken, it would be necessary to "lay down the law" to those department heads who resisted the acceptance of employees with obvious physical limitations but who were qualified for available jobs in the department.

Quite informally, a small committee of people with an active interest in such placement problems began meeting with the researcher who had been designated as project director. It included the industrial relations supervisor, who doubled as selective placement officer because of the strains created by the placement situation. Also included in this small committee were the safety director and the industrial physicians.

Under the existing procedures, there was resistance in various quarters to placement of employees with obvious physical impairments. First, the employee being placed was apt to be inwardly resistant to the assignment given him because the system provided little or no choice of jobs. Second, most department heads resisted the placement of such employees and regarded them as handicapped for the jobs in their units. Third, those department heads who cooperated with placement efforts soon discovered that they were getting a disproportionate share of the physically impaired and began to object to further placements.

The existing procedures were based on what has been called "a warped concept of physical fitness."[2] Fitness for industry and medical notions of fitness are quite different matters. A worker may not be able to do certain jobs or parts of jobs and yet be in excellent physical condition. On the other hand, a worker may require medical attention and still be fit to do any job in his department.

[2] Howard A. Rusk, M. D., and Henry Viscardi, Jr., *Hidden Sources of Manpower* (New York: American Management Association, 1952), p. 11.

The members of the small committee discussed placement practices in several companies in England, the United States and Canada. Some interest was shown in the placement procedures and organization then in use at the Ford Motor Company in Dearborn, Michigan. The organization consisted primarily of a team of placement officers each of whom was responsible for placements in a particular plant area for which he had detailed job knowledge. Ford's approach, it appeared, was an enlarged, better-organized version of that in use at Arvida.

The selective placement studies of the War Manpower Commission in the United States, as reported and developed by Clark Bridges,[3] were also considered. Alcan's chief medical officer, who was frequently brought into the discussions, suggested an examination of the selective placement forms and procedures as further developed and used by Hanman[4] to analyze the physical demands of jobs and to evaluate the physical capacities of men.

The Conceptual Model of a Placement System

Initially the goals of the Arvida placement project were to take care of the backlog of placement cases and to prevent future accumulations. In working out the conceptual model of a placement system, these twin objectives were recast in the form of a question: What means can be found to cope with changes in worker and job to ensure that each successive placement of an employee permits him to make the best use of his abilities which organizational, interpersonal, and health conditions permit?

In the beginning, the committee's work might best be described as model-building. As noted above, past practices were raked through; current ideas of managers and union people were mulled over; the practices of other companies were considered. In all this talk, the social subsystems of the Arvida community and plant were kept in the foreground. What difference did ethnic difference make? Or the difference between heavy and

[3] Clark D. Bridges, *Job Placement of the Physically Handicapped* (New York: McGraw-Hill Book Company, 1946).

[4] Bert Hanman, *Physical Capacities and Job Placement* (Stockholm: Nordisk Rotogravyr, 1951).

light industry? What was known about the jobs? What were
the administrative concerns of department heads with aging-
accident-illness problems? What was the extent and nature of
employee concern? And how was it reflected in community attitudes, or in the frequency and spacing of visits to plant physicians, or in absences from work? Which departments had the
most requests for transfers out?

In the turmoil of observations, opinions, and ideas the committee rediscovered for itself certain fundamentals of blue-collar
life which are important in designing a placement system. Notes
on committee meetings indicate that:

> Committee members recognized that a sudden reduction in
> an employee's physical capacity may undermine the net-
> work of his interpersonal relationships, on and off the job
> —relationships with work mates, friends and family. To a
> considerable extent, a man is what he does; his work situa-
> tion identifies him no less than his signature.
>
> Committee members felt that much of the force of aging-
> accident-illness problems is in their threat to meaningful
> roles, or the hope of finding some. For many, this hope
> turns on the continuing availability of some choice of job.
>
> It was noted that one of the frequent results of bigness in
> industry is some loss by the employee of control over the
> course of his work life. In the case of employees with ob-
> vious physical limitations, the exercise of positive self-di-
> rection in the area of work is apt to be greatly diminished.
>
> As a minimum such employees need some veto power over
> decisions affecting their work life. In this and other respects,
> those who have obvious physical impairments present a set
> of closely related problems, regardless of whether the im-
> pairments result from aging, or from accidents or illness.
> Since some amount of disability is everyone's problem now
> or later, a basis exists for broad employee support of efforts
> to devise a better placement system.[5]

Committee members agreed that it was pointless to cast the
problems which they set about solving in terms of financial

[5] These are excerpts from notes on committee discussions, September,
1954.

costs or returns to their employer. This disregard of money was never announced. To many it would have seemed both impractical and irresponsible, if not somehow a bit disloyal. Above all, it was purposeful and quite correct. The point was not to flout the rules of operation or to disregard the practical. Clearly, the model of the system being devised had to work. Money was somehow going to be involved, even though it appeared quite early that the money outlay for a sound system would *necessarily* be a minor matter. The important consideration in all this disregard of money was to establish a climate where innovation, and not bookkeeping, was the thing—a climate in which one could act independently of tough-minded "business considerations," and, if necessary, simply oppose them. For the work at hand, this approach placed the project outside the institutionalized conflicts of industry. Taken together with the lack of a special budget, this approach made the project *officially* unimportant, and added to the impression that not much was to be expected from it. In the early stages of the innovation, administrative disregard was far from an unmixed evil.

In the light of the fundamentals mentioned, the goals of the project came to be recast in the form of still another question: How might the bigness of the Arvida plant be put to work for better selective placement? In a series of committee discussions, the following conceptual elements of an improved selective placement system were advanced:

1. The system should serve the needs of the aging, as well as accident and sickness victims.
2. The new system should deal with abilities and not with disabilities of individual employees.
3. It should use efficiently for selective placement the generally high frequency of openings in a large plant due to employee separation or transfer. To do this, two co-ordinate kinds of information should be assembled and kept up to date. There should be a comprehensive, quantitative analysis of the physical demands of jobs and a correspondingly quantitative medical appraisal of the physical capacities of employees. The procedures for preparing profiles of man and job have

varied widely in complexity and quality. The purpose, however, has usually been the same—to bring worker and job together in a combination that allows the best use of the worker's skills and that agrees with him physically. The conceptual model of a placement system developed here omits discussion of procedures to determine employee skills, and skill requirements of jobs, and deals only with employee physical capacities and physical demands of jobs.

4. The aim should be grievance-free placement. This should be made possible by:

   a. Offering employees a choice of jobs.

   b. Insuring that an employee with an obvious physical impairment should not, on that account, be permitted to displace another with less service and who is physically fit, without that employee's consent. That is, the system should operate strictly on the basis of employee consent.

5. By making possible an early assignment to worth-while work, the new system should facilitate recovery of convalescent employees. It should reduce the danger of physical setback due to placement on jobs which might be too demanding.

6. The new system should include a light work department so that reduced-load assignments of convalescent employees to their regular jobs should be discontinued. This should make possible a truer picture of accident experience and general health condition of employees.

7. Better medical records should result, with more accurate projections of future placement needs, studies of the origin and distribution of transfer requests and of other phenomena of vital interest in placement work.

8. The new system was to be launched when enough jobs had been analyzed in all areas to permit selective placements to be distributed throughout the Works. This was seen as an important means to prevent doubt and misunderstanding among division heads and the hourly-paid, and to lay the basis for early expansion of the system to include all jobs in the Works.

9. In selective placement, the provision of a choice of jobs

would be the best way to affirm confidence in the individual's capacities and to buttress his image of self in his roles in the plant, in his family, and in the community. Offering a choice would be reassuring to the man during personal and family crises resulting from a disability. Such reassurance might actually reduce the handicapping effect of the impairment. Providing a choice might also contribute to the employee's acceptance of the job as the right one for him—one which he could do just as well as others who might lack his kind of physical limitations.

10. Whenever possible, the job choices should include one in the employee's own subdivision of the Works. This might serve the dual purposes of facilitating the employee's adjustment to the work group and, in accident cases, of raising the awareness of others around him to the need for safety precautions.

11. For employees with permanent impairments, one or more jobs should be found which are paid at rates that are at least equal to that of the previous job. While this may not be possible in some instances, there ought not to be a decrease in mean rates from old jobs to new. In job evaluation procedures, the relatively low weight assigned to working conditions and physical effort makes this feasible inasmuch as the impaired employee usually has skills which might be utilized to offset his disability.

Selective placement is an awkward term and a misleading one. It smacks of power over others and manipulation. It has been used to refer to various kinds of procedures for matching the physical capacities of workers to the physical demands of jobs. Conceivably, a procedure may be turned into an instrument of domination in the hands of a martinet. The model presented here was designed as an employee-centered or *mutual* approach to vital problems. As such, it leaves little room for the manipulations of a martinet or for individuals or groups in the plant to claim a benefactor role. Mutuality means development of the system on the basis of general interest in the common human problems arising from aging, accident and illness.

Survey of the Works

At the same time that various selective placement procedures were being examined, action was begun on the first committee decision. This was to survey the Works for approximately seventy jobs on which physically impaired workers might be placed. These were to be widely distributed horizontally in the plant and vertically in terms of skill and pay. In part, it was hoped, this survey would turn up some quick answers to some of the more urgent placement problems and at the same time start the progressive development of a long-range placement system.

With agreement on the survey, the problem arose of people who could work effectively on the project and provide the project director with job information not otherwise available. This problem was discussed informally with committee members and with the personnel manager who, after various candidates had been considered, suggested that several safety inspectors be asked to spend part of their time on the project. On the basis of the services performed by the safety inspectors, their knowledge of the plant, and their social and psychological identification with the work force, three safety inspectors were chosen.

During September, 1954, the committee was an informal discussion group of interested plant people. Early in October, a project committee was formally constituted with eight of the most interested and creative members of the informal group. Occupationally, the committee was made up as follows:

Occupational position	Number
Acting selective placement officer[6]	1
Safety director	1
Safety inspector	3
Staff physician	2
Research associate (Staff Training and Research Division, Montreal)	1

[6] The acting selective placement officer at the time had the title of industrial relations supervisor. However, the difficulties surrounding the backlog of selective placement cases occupied a very substantial part of his time.

Later the employment manager was added to the committee. From time to time the chief medical officer of the company, Montreal, took part in project committee meetings.

The organization of the survey was based on safety zones. Job descriptions provided by the Industrial Engineering Department were studied, and from these, tentative lists of jobs to be considered were compiled by safety zones. Thereafter each safety inspector on the committee teamed up in turn with the project director to go over the list for his zone. Contrary to management opinion, it soon appeared that the descriptions drawn up by the industrial engineers provided little reliable information on the *physical* demands of the jobs. All lists were drastically revised in discussions with the safety inspectors on the committee.

The next phase of the survey followed immediately. It consisted of actual observations of the jobs and discussions with the incumbent about the requirements of his job and the purposes of the survey. Within several weeks the survey was finished and its results reviewed by the committee and put to the service of the acting selective placement officer.

This survey was valuable in several ways:

1. It demonstrated that conventional job descriptions made by industrial engineers in evaluating jobs for pay purposes were of very little value in placing the physically impaired.
2. It convinced committee members that descriptions of jobs for placement purposes by such subjective terms as "light" or "heavy" were of little value.
3. It identified for use in selective placement many jobs that had previously been judged too difficult by placement people who casually accepted work-world myths.
4. Above all, it established the need for analyzing the physical demands of jobs in specific and reliable terms. It was decided to follow the lead given by the War Manpower Commission, Bridges,[7] and Hanman.[8] The latter's version of a physical de-

---

[7] *Op. cit.*
[8] *Op. cit.*

mands analysis work sheet was adapted for use at Arvida
Works (see Figure 2).

5. The survey work became the testing ground for new ideas
   by committee members about how a selective placement
   system might be developed and installed.

6. Finally, talking to job incumbents about aging-accident-illness
   problems convincingly showed that a rational system of selective placement would most certainly serve deep and funda-
   mental needs of the hourly paid.

Learning to Analyze Physical Demands

The project committee next considered the role of job analyst
in the plant. It discussed training for the work of job analysis,
and the analyst's communication responsibilities to the man on
the job, the foreman and others.

The question arose of using industrial engineers to analyze
jobs. They offered their help and had previously contributed
important material for understanding the situation in the janitor
service. After some discussion the project committee concluded
that selective placement involves basically different problems
from those that are central to industrial engineering. True, the
determination of physical and environmental demands of jobs
involves procedures which are superficially similar to job study
by industrial engineers. The differences, however, are funda-
mental and concern aims and consequences which have nothing
to do with job evaluation for pay purposes.

It was decided that in the beginning the project director
should team up with each of the three safety inspectors and the
acting selective placement officer to analyze jobs. Thereafter,
each analyst was to be paired in turn with each of the other analysts. It was planned that later each would work alone on a quota
of jobs. Each analyst familiarized himself generally with the
definitions of job factors developed by Bridges, Hanman, and
others (see Appendix II). The committee put out its own direc-
tives on how the work was to be approached in the Works and
how the aims were to be presented to job incumbents and others.

Each pair of analysts reported to the foreman, explained care-

Job # *1812*

PHYSICAL DEMANDS ANALYSIS WORK SHEET

Job Title: _Senior Aluminum Operator_

Job Location: _Potrooms_

Physical Factors:

1	1	1– 5	
2	2	6– 10	
½	3	11– 25	Lifting (Pounds)— Includes pushing and pulling effort while stationary
½	4	26– 50	
¼	5	51–100	
	6	100+	
½	7	1– 5	
1	8	6– 10	
¼	9	11– 25	Carrying (Pounds)— Includes pushing and pulling effort while walking
¼	10	26– 50	
¼	11	51–100	
	12	100+	
	13	R	Fingering
	14	L	
4	15	R	Handling
4	16	L	
3½	17	R	Below Shoulders
3½	18	L	
½	19	R	Above Shoulders
½	20	L	Reaching
½	21	R	Throwing
½	22	L	
4	23	Sitting	
3½	24	Total Time on Feet	
3	25	Standing	
½	26	Walking	
	27	Running	
	28	Jumping	
	29	Legs Only	Climbing
	30	Legs and Arms	
	31	R	While Sitting
	32	L	
	33	R	While Standing	Treading
	34	L	
3	35	Stooping	
½	36	Crouching	
	37	Kneeling	
	38	Crawling	
	39	Reclining	
4	40	Twisting	
4	41	Waiting Time	

20/30	42	Far—Snellen	
6	43	Near—Jaeger	Seeing
	44	Color	
+	45	Depth	
+	46	Hearing	
+	47	Talking	
	48	Other:	
	49	Other:	

Environmental Factors:

8	50	Inside	
	51	Fair Weather	
	52	Wet Weather	Outside
¼	53	Hot °F 115	
	54	Cold °F	
	55	Sudden Temperature Changes	
	56	Humid	
	57	Dry	
	58	Moving Objects	
	59	Hazardous Machinery	
	60	Hazardous Tools or Materials	
	61	Cluttered Floors	
	62	Slippery Floors	
	63	High Places	
	64	Electrical Hazards	
4	65	Exposure to Burns	
4	66	Explosives	
	67	Radiant Energy (Kind):	
	68	Poor Lighting	
4	69	Poor Ventilation	
4	70	Toxic Conditions (Kind): Hydrofluoric acid, carbon monoxide	
	71	Wet Quarters	
4	72	Close Quarters	
	73	Vibration	
	74	Noise	
	75	Working With Others	
	76	Working Around Others	
4	77	Working Alone	
D	78	Shifts	
	79	Other:	
	80	Other:	

J. Tremblay
Job Analyst's Name

T. Paris
Verified with: Foreman's Name

May 20, 1965
Date

FIGURE 2. *Physical Demands Analysis Work Sheet*

fully the nature and purposes of the analysis, and then talked with the man on the job. Aging-accident-illness problems were presented as the concern of everyone. Yet, it was pointed out, no one had advanced any very good answers to the placement needs that were bound to arise sooner or later for everyone. No claim was made, except that new and serious efforts were being undertaken to work out better approaches. It was also pointed out that nothing would be done to change the practice of trying to keep employees who required selective placement, within their departments and sections. Moreover, it was explained that the project had nothing to do with wage rates and was in no way related to any efforts to increase work loads. In general, job analysis was presented as serving common needs. It was hoped that this would be just as apparent to the worker from the analysts' manner as from the things which were said. The analysts worked without stint, performing a great many of the job operations regardless of the difficulties or hazards for someone who had not been initiated properly to the nature of the job. By this kind of contact with the job incumbent, questions were answered and job elements were demonstrated.

The analysts, after thanking the worker for his help, returned to the department or section office where each independently filled out a work sheet (see Figure 2 above). At various points, questions arose between the analysts or between an analyst and the foreman regarding some detail of the job that was unclear. When both work sheets were finished, the judgments for all eighty items of the work sheet were compared. Where points of difference existed, a discussion followed until agreement was reached on one consolidated work sheet.

Before signing the work sheet, the foreman usually had questions on the analysis. He wanted to know how one or another estimate was reached. Many times such a question sent the analysts back to the job incumbent for more information. The result was greatly increased job knowledge and more effective handling of all kinds of job changes throughout the Works.

In the first weeks of job analysis, the project committee meetings were largely concerned with discussions of problems that developed on different types of jobs; for example, one analyst team would describe some part of the duties, such as a material issuer in the central warehouse, and then ask the others how they would handle that problem on a work sheet. Thus the discussions developed around concrete problems of analyzing the physical and environmental demands of particular jobs. By this means and by the rotation of analysts so that everyone had at some time worked with everyone else, analysts shared their new skills with each other and developed a common frame of reference for dealing with recurrent problems.

The Teams Continue

After several weeks of job analysis on a part-time basis, it seemed to the project director that the analysts enjoyed the teamwork. It was decided, however, to place on the committee agenda a discussion of the advisability of starting individual work. This would mean doubling the number of jobs that could be analyzed simultaneously. Since there was no budgetary provision for the new work of job analysis, this had to be added to the normal work load of committee members, with no increase in pay. Despite the prospect of halving the hours of extra work, some objection to breaking up the teams was expected. The result was unanimous disapproval. The arguments were based on "quality of the analysis," "response by the man on the job," and "better discussions with the foreman." In addition, the job analysts made it clear that teamwork added interest. They were not so sure the work would proceed much faster on an individual basis. They were certain it would be less accurate and communication with the work force would be less successful. On the strength of these arguments, the committee decided that the teams should continue.

In the spring of 1955, job analysis was continued on a part-time basis by the safety inspectors. When more than eighty jobs had been analyzed, the analysts reported self-critically that they had departed somewhat from the list projected at the end of the plant survey. They felt that the distribution of the jobs which had been analyzed was not good enough, either by plant area or skill and pay. They recommended that about forty additional jobs should be analyzed before the formal launching of the new system. Additionally, they undertook the extra work on the same volunteer basis as before, while carrying on their regular safety inspection duties. They once again overfulfilled their self-assigned quota to a total of 130 jobs.

Special Communication Questions

From the beginning of the project, concern was expressed in the committee about building and maintaining rapport with employees—from the hourly paid to superintendents. Attention to communication problems meant that every member of the committee was actually involved in administrative aspects of the project as well as the details of job analysis. Explanations had to be adequate for a senior manager and, more important, analysts had to answer the implied, as well as the expressed, questions of the hourly paid.

Early in the job analysis work, a question arose on communication policy. The editor of *Le Lingot*, Alcan's local newspaper distributed free to employees, suggested an interview with the project director for a series of articles "to explain the project to employees at all levels." The proposal was taken to the project committee for discussion.

The differences between formal and informal communications were considered. Mention was made of such formal means as circular letters, with specified distributions, as well as *Le Lingot*, and the ways in which formal communications are "re-edited" by the reader to fit his definition of company interests, and then passed on informally. It seemed to the committee members that both formal and informal means could reinforce each other and help the project. It also seemed to committee members that reliance, in the early stages of the project, had to be on the informal means, however time-consuming. The proposal for the series of articles was turned down. Among the objections to such a series was one that such publicity would tend to generate employee expectations which it might not be possible to fulfill. Instead, it was decided to rely on circular letters (see letter dated November 22, 1954, in Appendix III) which would give weight to the company's commitment without generating premature hopes that might well boomerang against the committee.

The Committee Work of the Staff Physicians

As job analysis increasingly became a routine matter, discussions turned toward the practical problems faced by the medical staff. The defects of the old placement system were keenly felt by nurses and physicians alike. They were regularly asked to do the impossible. Without real job knowledge, they were in effect called on to decide about the fitness of men to work on particular jobs. The physicians' judgments were challenged by managers and workers. The only translation of diagnostic data into something at all meaningful to a layman was the PULHEMS rating of an employee.

Under this system, the findings of a physical examination are summarized by giving a rating of 1, 2, 3 or 4 (meaning excellent, average, moderate or below minimum standards) for each of the following:

P — Physical capacity or stamina
U — Upper extremities
L — Lower extremities
H — Head
E — Ears and eyesight
M — Mental component
S — Neuro-psychiatric component

Summarizing diagnostic information this way is not very helpful to the layman in placement. He needs competent judgments of the physical and environmental capacities of employees, stated in time units, so that he can match capacities with job demands, stated in the same standard units.

Experience in selective placement work using PULHEMS appraisals of workers and industrial engineering appraisals of jobs was poor. Hardly anyone had confidence in the system, and aggrieved employees went back to the physicians again and again to describe their conditions and to explain why they could not continue on the jobs selected for them. Managers, too, disagreed frequently with the physicians. The physician's position was difficult for the following reasons: rarely could he know the physical demands of jobs; under his code, diagnostic information was supposed to be kept confidential; and there were no specific terms by which to describe an employee's capacities to laymen for their use in selective placement.

One source of strain between medical personnel and the safety director and other department heads, was placement of convalescent employees. The safety department was eager for the return of employees as early in their convalescence as possible. The practice was to permit employees who were still convalescing to return to their old jobs, allowing them to undertake less than a normal work load. This provided the employee with his regular full income and reduced the workmen's compensation rate or the company's disability payments. These "part-job" assignments were difficult to administer, had unfavorable effects on relations in work groups, and occasionally may have delayed employees' physical recovery. In any case, conflict tended to develop between the industrial physicians, primarily concerned with the recovery of their patients, and members of the safety department.

The strains between the physicians and other department people were mentioned at various times in the project committee. As the discussion developed during and between meetings, agreement emerged on the following points:

1. There was a serious need to make available to laymen working in placement more detailed and specific information than that provided by PULHEMS ratings. It was decided to follow the lead of the War Manpower Commission, Bridges[9] and Hanman,[10] adapting the latter's version of a physical capacities report form (see Figure 3).
2. While an objection could be made that no translation of diagnostic data into physical capacities was possible in exact

[9] *Op cit.*
[10] *Op. cit.*

PHYSICAL CAPACITIES REPORT

Blank Spaces = Full Capacity.   Numbers = Hours of Partial Capacity.   O = No Capacity

Name of Employee *J. V. Murphy* .... Number *6572*

Male *✓* .... Female .... Date of Birth *July 1, 1916* Height *5' 3"* Weight *138*

Physical Factors:

	1	1— 5
	2	6— 10
	3	11— 25
2	4	26— 50
1	5	51—100
0	6	100+

Lifting (Pounds)— Includes pushing and pulling effort while stationary

	7	1— 5
	8	6— 10
	9	11— 25
1	10	26— 50
1/2	11	51—100
0	12	100+

Carrying (Pounds)— Includes pushing and pulling effort while walking

	13	R
	14	L

Fingering

	15	R
	16	L

Handling

	17	R
	18	L

Below Shoulders

	19	R
	20	L

Above Shoulders

Reaching

	21	R
	22	L

Throwing

•	23	Sitting
4	24	Total Time on Feet
4	25	Standing
2	26	Walking
0	27	Running
0	28	Jumping
1/2	29	Legs Only
0	30	Legs and Arms

Climbing

	31	R
0	32	L

While Sitting

2	33	R
2	34	L

While Standing

Treading

	35	Stooping
0	36	Crouching
0	37	Kneeling
0	38	Crawling
	39	Reclining
	40	Twisting
	41	Waiting Time

	42	Far—Snellen
2	43	Near—Jaeger
	44	Color
	45	Depth

Seeing

	46	Hearing
	47	Talking
	48	Other: ....
	49	Other: ....

Environmental Factors:

	50	Inside
	51	Fair Weather
	52	Wet Weather

Outside

	53	Hot °F ....
	54	Cold °F ....
O	55	Sudden Temperature Changes
	56	Humid
	57	Dry
	58	Moving Objects
	59	Hazardous Machinery
	60	Hazardous Tools or Materials
	61	Cluttered Floors
O	62	Slippery Floors
O	63	High Places
	64	Electrical Hazards
	65	Exposure To Burns
	66	Explosives
	67	Radiant Energy (Kind): ....
	68	Poor Lighting
	69	Poor Ventilation
O	70	Toxic Conditions (Kind): ....
	71	Wet Quarters
	72	Close Quarters
	73	Vibration
	74	Noise
	75	Working With Others
	76	Working Around Others
	77	Working Alone
	78	Shifts
	79	Other: ....
	80	Other: ....

Physician's Remarks *(on physician's copy only)*
Mild bronchitis. Left leg amputated below knee.

Date *July 8, 1965* Physician's Name *W. W. Smith*

FIGURE 3. *Physical Capacities Report*

terms at the existing level of medical knowledge, placement always involved such a translation. Moreover, it was better to have a physician make the translation, than a placement officer without medical training.

3. Better placement of aging-accident-illness cases could bring about a greatly improved situation in the plant, which might also reduce somewhat the difficulties of the medical services.

Among the questions brought before the committee were the following: How might the physicians be trained to prepare physical capacities reports? How might it be possible to arrive at a common frame of reference in preparing them? The safety inspectors, who had become job analysts, gave the answer to this indirectly by their successful experience with teamwork in preparing the job analyses. Alcan's chief physician volunteered to work with each of the industrial physicians in doing the initial physical capacities reports on employees.

As the physicians became more familiar with the mechanics of the system being developed, their commitment to it grew. There was particular satisfaction in the fact that they were making available to placement people all the information and judgments which they could possibly use. At the same time, the new procedures removed any seeming justification for disclosing confidential medical information on workers to people in management.

One further satisfaction of the physicians with the emerging system was that selective placement decisions would rest where they properly belonged—with the placement personnel in the employment office.

The First Placements

From the beginning of the project, committee members became aware that there were certain individuals whose placement problems were the subject of widespread interest and concern by employees. There was an atmosphere of skeptical questioning about such cases. One heard such queries as "What will happen to George?" Often, this kind of question was put more bluntly: "What will the company do about George?" The general question-form of employee concern was "What will they do about George?" No one seemed to wonder whether anyone really knew what could be done about "George" or how it could be done. The common assumption seemed to be that the only thing missing was a proper intent—that the "what" and "how" were known. The we-and-they structuring of relationships in industry was particularly manifest in references to disabled employees. It became increasingly clear to the committee that one of its communication tasks was to make clear that so far *no one* really had a sound, comprehensive set of answers to placement in aging-accident-illness cases. If nobody had adequate answers, who could object to the efforts of the committee? This formulation also helped to head off premature hopes of employees for the quick solution of the accumulated problems.

The committee decided that in its first placement efforts, it would carefully and quietly solve some of those key cases, leaving it to the grapevine to announce the results. These first placement efforts cannot be described here, but they were successful, and favorable comments were heard in widely separated parts of the plant. By the time of the formal launching of Arvida's mutual system of placement a few such crucial placements had already been made.

The Launching

On June 1, 1955, a circular letter signed by the employment manager was issued. It announced simply that in previous months the physical requirements of various occupations in the plant had been studied with the aim of enlarging the number of possible locations where employees with physical impairments might work. It added that "employees requesting transfers for reasons of physical unfitness and employees returning from absences due to illness or injury are being examined medically, and new procedures are being used to evaluate their physical capacities rather than their limitations." The letter announced that a safety inspector would act as coordinator of the selective placement program under the jurisdiction of the employment manager, and that the "coordinator's immediate responsibilities will consist of exploring the possibilities of suitable placement for some forty employees who have been medically examined recently and whose physical capacities do not match the requirements of their present jobs."

Arvida's mutual approach to selective placement began as a limited system, with only 130 of the nearly 400 jobs (as then defined) analyzed. Progressive inclusion of all hourly paid jobs was foreseen and was built into the administration of the limited system in anticipation of company approval. By October, 1956, under the direction of the coordinator of the new system, the expansion was complete: all jobs in the Works had been analyzed.

The Kitimat Project

In the summer of 1958, the research associate who had served as director of the Arvida project spent three weeks at Alcan's Kitimat Works, Kitimat, British Columbia, helping to adapt and extend the Arvida system to this plant, which began operation in 1954. In the limited time available, a series of discussions were held with plant people who later constituted the project committee. Two employees were trained to do job analyses, and twenty jobs were analyzed. Preliminary discussions were held on several long-standing placement cases. In sum, the minimum organizational and training steps were taken for the development of a placement system on the Arvida model. By June, 1960, all jobs in Kitimat Works and in the Kemano powerhouse 50 miles away had been analyzed and a new placement system was in full operation.

The Arvida and Kitimat plants represent sharply contrasting situations. The chief element they have in common is that the primary product at each location is aluminum ingot. While Arvida's hourly paid work force is homogeneously native-born, French-Canadian and Catholic, Kitimat's ethnic-religious composition is decidedly heterogeneous. When the placement project was begun, Kitimat Works had just half as many jobs and half as many hourly paid workers as Arvida. These ratios at present show little change. Further, the Kitimat work force is young by almost any industrial standard; Arvida's is fairly old. The difference in the mean age is slightly more than eight years. In addition, the rates of labor turnover are markedly different: Kitimat, being a relatively new and isolated community, tends to attract employees for short periods of employment, unlike Arvida which contains a predominantly stable population.

When the committee was formed for the Kitimat project, its members had available to them the first report on Arvida's mutual system. Furthermore, the extension of the system was encouraged by Alcan's director of personnel (see letter dated January 10, 1958, in Appendix III). These circumstances added to the contrasts with Arvida noted above. At Arvida, every member of the project committee worked with a certain felt inadequacy. No one knew quite where the project was going, and little was expected of it. At Kitimat, budgetary and organizational provisions were made even before there was a committee. The project was officially important. In Arvida the project committee was, by circumstances, an instrument for innovation in the fullest sense; it was a working committee to which everyone brought his own special competence, but where no one "knew the answers." In Kitimat, no one doubted that the thing to do was to adapt and extend the Arvida system. The questions taken up by the Kitimat committee were more often administrative than substantive. The organizational approaches were essentially the same as at Arvida.

The one big hazard facing the Kitimat committee was the variety of languages spoken in the plant. German and Portuguese had approximately the same number of users. The job analysts spoke only English. Communication, it was agreed, had to be mainly by word-of-mouth in the early stages. The committee considered a variety of means of insuring clear supporting communication within the ethnic groups at the Works. The situational pressures in the new plant, however, precluded their organized use. Significantly, there have been no ill effects of this omission. It would seem that the manner in which the carefully chosen analysts did their work and the emphasis at all times on the needs of the hourly paid in aging-accident-illness matters, spoke clearly without the need for interpreters. It is also likely that there was favorable interplant communication between Arvida and Kitimat at the hourly paid level.

Summary

How did the Arvida project committee work? What was its
relationship to senior management and to the union? The project
committee started with a clean slate. No one had an answer to
the problems it faced. No one seemed to expect much from the
committee. It operated without a budget and without official
standing in the organization.

The union[11] was not formally consulted, though explanations
of committee intentions were personally made to many hundreds
of union members, and active account was taken of the concerns
of leaders and rank and file facing placement problems. The
only formality observed in dealing with the union was a meeting
held before the plan was launched, at which time the plan was
explained.

The mutual approach to placement was developed in informal
seminar-type discussions of the committee. In regard to skills,
the committee was self-taught. Working in pairs, the members
learned job analysis. Initially, the physicians worked in close consultation to prepare physical capacities report forms on the first
employees to be placed under the new system. Since the mass
media of communication were not used for explanations to employees, the committee threshed out the problems in person-to-
person communication. Finally, in the performance of these
varied tasks, there emerged the skills to administer the system.

The committee was composed of people with roles which were
known to be acceptable to employees at all levels. Included was
a sociologist, on loan to the plant from head office, who helped
to plan and execute the several phases of the project, including
a survey of the Works, and job analysis.

The uncommon zest with which the safety inspectors and the
other project people did their work suggests that the committee
had various latent functions for its members. It provided new
experience, work that was socially meaningful and recognition
from others whom they esteemed but who exercised no formal

---

[11] The reference is to Syndicat national des employés de l'aluminium
d'Arvida. The production employees at Kitimat Works have a local of the
United Steelworkers of America.

authority over them. And most important, some of their own deep-seated needs were met by organized work on the aging-accident-illness problems of others. They got something which is not for sale by insurance companies. In the responses of committee members and of the employees generally, one may see how the individual draws support from a social approach to social problems.

While the committee's work formally ended with the launching of the system, "committee work" is still an intermittent feature of Arvida's mutual system of placement. Formal and informal consultation with members of the founding project committee has continued. In some form, committee work is clearly a requirement for the effective operation of the system and the solution of the new problems that regularly arise.

The development of a placement system at Kitimat provides a certain perspective with which to view the founding of the mutual system at Arvida. The Kitimat project was assisted by the fact of the Arvida experience, but this experience was not an unmixed blessing. At Arvida the lack of ready answers was, in an important sense, an advantage in the development phase. At Kitimat, situational pressures suggested "short cuts." There was resistance to committee discussion of job analysis since everyone was said to be "familiar with the Arvida experiences." It quickly became apparent that it was no short cut to reduce or eliminate committee discussion. In the long run, such discussion proved to be as important as the mechanics of the system.

What bearing does this have on the development of mutual systems in other plants? Clearly, there is a place for committee work; it has to do somewhat the same things that were done in Arvida in the fall and winter of 1954-55, and in Kitimat in 1958. It has to facilitate the development of skills, the co-ordination of interests, and the generation of new ideas, to meet new problems of communication and organization.

3. The Mutual System of Placement (MSP): Procedures and Organization

Three basic tools are used for selective placement under the mutual system. One of these is the physical demands analysis work sheet (see Figure 2, above); another, the physical capacities report (see Figure 3, above), which is referred to here as an M-3. As described previously, a physical demands work sheet is prepared for each job by a job analyst; physical capacities reports (M-3's) are prepared for employees by physicians.

It will be clear at a glance that these two forms resemble each other in that each lists 80 job factors, divided into physical factors (numbers 1 to 49) and environmental factors (50 to 80). In filling out an M-3, the physician provides a set of specific answers to the general question: What is this employee physically able to do? In filling out a physical demands work sheet, the job analyst provides a set of specific answers to the general question: What is physically required in order to do this job? With the two sets of answers, stated in the same units, and juxtaposed (forms prepared for actual use in placement are printed so that boxes match up), one can see in a moment whether the physician's estimates of an employee's capacities come within the demands of a job.

In most instances a master chart is used in placing employees. This is the third basic tool of the mutual system of placement (MSP). It is simply a loose-leaf compilation of information from the physical demands work sheets. The data for each job occupy a single column, with the job title entered in the diagonal area above the column (see Figure 4). The Arvida master chart is organized by departments[1] because efforts are usually made to place a man with some kind of impairment in his own department. The name of the department and/or division is entered at the top of the sheet of the master chart.

Maintaining the Master Chart

Just as jobs change, so must the master chart. The mutual system of placement (MSP) was begun with 130 selected jobs in the first master chart. In the summer of 1956, the analysis of the physical demands of jobs was resumed on a part-time basis by the placement officer and one safety inspector. By October, the remaining 270 jobs were included in the master chart, making a total for the plant of 400.

Since 1956, many jobs have changed in both physical and environmental demands.[2] Changes in job content were reflected in an increase in the number of jobs from 400 in October, 1956, to 520 four years later, an increase of 30 per cent. This increase came about through reorganization of jobs by the industrial engineers as much as by technological change. Curiously, even the combining of jobs tends, in a complex plant, to increase the number of jobs. Some examples may make this clear:

In Ore Plant 2, the jobs of scales operator[3] and evaporating

---

[1] After each department or division grouping of jobs in the master chart, a summary column is provided. In it is recorded, by inspection, the highest physical demand on each factor for all jobs in the grouping. Clearly, if a man can meet the demands recorded in this summary column, he then is physically qualified for any job in the grouping. From the summary columns of the various job groupings in the master chart it is a simple matter to prepare a summary column for the Works. With a well-maintained master chart, a periodic examination of summary columns of department, division and Works can provide a picture of changes in the physical demands of jobs that may (or may not) accompany changes in technology and work organization.

[2] The term environmental demands is an awkward one since part of the demands or effects of environment are experienced immediately as physical demands. Other effects may be equally physical and immediate but the experience of them may be delayed.

[3] The names of jobs are those used by the Syndicate (union) and management. No clarification is provided for the reader because an understanding of job details is without importance for understanding the other material.

MASTER CHART
PHYSICAL AND ENVIRONMENTAL DEMANDS

Job Titles — Job Locations — Job Numbers

Mechanical Division
Machine Shop

Numbers = Maximum Hours Required
+ = Required
E = Either Right or Left
Blank Spaces = Not Required

Page	SUMMARY COLUMN	Machinist (2)	Machinist (1)	Helper trades	Fitter Cl.3	Fitter Cl.2	Fitter Cl.1	Craneman	Lifting (Pounds) — Includes pushing and pulling effort while stationary
1	6	2	2	1	3	3	3	6	1— 5
2	3	½	½	3	3	3	3	1	6— 10
3	2	½	½	1	2	2	2		11— 25
4	1	½	½	½	½	½	½		26— 50
5	½	½	½						51—100
6	¼							¼	100+

Page	SUMMARY COLUMN	Machinist (2)	Machinist (1)	Helper trades	Fitter Cl.3	Fitter Cl.2	Fitter Cl.1	Craneman	Carrying (Pounds) — Includes pushing and pulling effort while walking
7	½	1	1	½	½	1½	1½		1— 5
8	½	¼	¼	1½	1½	1½	1½		6— 10
9	1	¼	¼	½	1	1	1		11— 25
10	½	¼	¼	½	¼	¼	¼		26— 50
11	¼	¼	¼	¼					51—100
12	¼							¼	100+12

Physical Factors																																		
Fingering	R	13					1½				1½				1½								1				1					1½	13
Fingering	L	14					1½				1½				1½								1				1					1½	14
Handling	R	15	7				4½				4½				4½				6				4				4					7	15
Handling	L	16	7				4½				4½				4½				6				4				4					7	16
Reaching – Below Shoulders	R	17	7				6				6				6				6				3				3					7	17
Reaching – Below Shoulders	L	18	7				6				6				6				6				3				3					7	18
Reaching – Above Shoulders	R	19	¼																				½				½					½	19
Reaching – Above Shoulders	L	20	¼																				1				1					1	20
Throwing	R	21					1				1				1				1				½				½					1	21
Throwing	L	22					1				1				1				1				½				½					1	22
Sitting		23	7																				4				4					7	23
Total Time on Feet		24	½				6				6				6				6				4				4					6	24
Standing		25					5½				5½				5½				5½				½				½					5½	25
Walking		26	½				½				½				½				½													½	26
Running		27																															27
Jumping		28																															28
Climbing – Legs Only		29																															29
Climbing – Legs and Arms		30	¼																¼													¼	30
Treading – While Sitting	R	31	3																													3	31
Treading – While Sitting	L	32	3																													3	32
Treading – While Standing	R	33																															33
Treading – While Standing	L	34																															34
Stooping		35	4				3				3				3				3				2				2					4	35
Crouching		36					2				2				2				1													2	36
Kneeling		37					1				1				1				½													1	37
Crawling		38																															38
Reclining		39																															39
Twisting		40	7				6				6				6				6				4				4					7	40
Waiting Time		41	1				2				2				2				2				4				4					4	41

Physical Factors

FIGURE 4. *Master Chart*

[Continued on next page]

MASTER CHART

PHYSICAL AND ENVIRONMENTAL DEMANDS

Numbers=Maximum Hours Required
+ =Required
E=Either Right or Left
Blank Spaces=Not Required

Job Titles — Job Locations — Job Numbers
Mechanical Division
Machine Shop

Page

Seeing / Demand		#	Craneman	Fitter Cl.1	Fitter Cl.2	Fitter Cl.3	Helper Trades	Machinist (1)	Machinist (2)	SUMMARY COLUMN
Seeing	Far — Snellen	42	20/30	20/30	20/30	20/30	20/30	20/30	20/30	20/30
	Near — Jaeger	43	9	2	2	2	2	2	2	2
	Color	44	+	+	+	+	+	+	+	+
	Depth	45	+	+	+	+	+	+	+	+
	Hearing	46	+	+	+	+	+	+	+	+
	Talking	47	+	+	+	+	+	+	+	+
	Other	48								
	Other	49								
	Inside	50	8	5	5	5	8	8	8	8
Outside	Fair Weather	51								
	Wet Weather	52		1	1	1				1
	Hot .....°F	53								
	Cold .....F°	54								
	Sudden Temperature Changes	55								
	Humid	56								
	Dry	57								

FIGURE 4. *Master Chart—continued*

Environmental Factors		1131	1105	1224	1107	1368	1430	1472
Moving Objects	58	7						7
Hazardous Machinery	59							4
Sharp Tools or Materials	60						4	4
Cluttered Floors	61							
Slippery Floors	62							
High Places	63	1/4				1/4		1/4
Electrical Hazards	64							
Exposure to Burns	65		3	3	3	1/4		3
Explosives	66		3	3	3	1/4		3
Radiant Energy	67							
Poor Lighting	68							
Poor Ventilation	69	7						7
Toxic Conditions	70	7						7
Wet Quarters	71							
Close Quarters	72							
Vibration	73	7				1/2		7
Noise	74					1/2		1/2
Working With Others	75		8	8	8	8		8
Working Around Others	76	7	8	8	8	8	8	8
Working Alone	77							
Shifts	78	5	D,S	D,S	D,S	5	5	D,S
Other:	79							
Other:	80							
Job Numbers →		1131	1105	1224	1107	1368	1430	1472

unit operator were combined; in Ore Plant 1, they remained separate. Result: An increase from two jobs to three for the Works.

The same pattern was repeated in the same way and with the same result for the jobs of digester operator and classifier operator.

A new job, pot operator, was created by combining the jobs of trimmer and crust breaker operator on the Soderberg pot lines but not in the prebake pot lines. Result: An increase from two jobs to three for the Works.

Part of the increase of 30 per cent was due to improper lumping of jobs in preparing the first master chart at Arvida. By separating them, new placement possibilities were brought to light that were previously obscured.

The basic procedure for analyzing the physical demands of jobs is the one set forth in Chapter II, which requires a close working relationship between:

1. The analyst(s) and the man on the job and, thereafter, for purposes of checking, between
2. The analyst(s) and the foreman and perhaps other supervisory personnel.

Because of the frequency of job changes, it was not always possible with the available help to re-analyze jobs as fast as necessary. Because of the system requirement to keep up with the work of revising the master chart, it sometimes happened that insufficient time was spent with the job incumbent. One outcome of this was the occasional reappearance of the results of narrow departmental thinking, expressed in the overstatement of the physical demands of jobs. This reduced temporarily the number of placement possibilities in the department and, therefore, the number of in-transfers. Five years after launching MSP, a full revision of the master chart was carried out. Since then, continuous revision is standard practice.

New Procedures

In the spring of 1960, means were considered to reduce the loss of selective placement opportunities through casual and ill-advised transfers of employees. Procedures were devised to improve the collection of information on needs and openings.

The main feature of this procedure is a simplified report, supplied monthly to each department, on the physical match of men and jobs for all employees in the department. The purpose of the report is to classify employees according to the degree of need for transfer to other work.

The procedure used is as follows: M-3's are completed routinely by physicians, either when new employees are hired or during periodic examinations of employees on the payroll. As M-3's reach the placement officer the employee's physical capacities are summarized according to the following categories:

1. Full physical; full environmental
2. Limited physical; full environmental
3. Full physical; limited environmental
4. Selective placement case (not to be displaced without consulting employment office)
5. Placement to be made (serious placement problem).

By comparing the M-3 of the employee with the demands of his job and with those of his department and "promotional seniority area,"[4] *guiding* recommendations to departments are worked out according to the following categories:

1. Stay in present work and location
2. Stay in present work only
3. Stay in present location only
4. Placement to be made at once
5. Placement to be made at first opportunity
6. Placement to be made soon.

[4] A "promotional seniority area" consists of those jobs to which an employee with the necessary seniority and competence may be promoted.

In addition to the preceding information the employees' basic service data are supplied along with the dates of the last physical examination and the next scheduled one.

It is important to emphasize that the purpose of the monthly reports is to reduce as much as possible the strain and waste of unwise transfer efforts; selective placement is the responsibility of the selective placement officer. The basic tools remain the M-3, the master chart and the physical demands work sheets from which it is compiled.

An employee whose physical capacities no longer meet the demands of his job comes to the selective placement officer in one of the following ways:

1. By the employee's own action. He may request placement either directly or through his foreman.
2. By action of a manager:
   (a) In promoting or demoting employees;
   (b) In transferring employees during a layoff;
   (c) In the case of obvious physical impairment, but when the employee fails to act.
3. By action of the medical staff.

A serious accident or illness always involves comparison of the physical demands of jobs and the capacities of the worker. An M-3 is filled out at the time of an employee's regular examination, as well as at the time he returns from a serious illness or accident. The selective placement officer gets a copy of all M-3's. Either a recent M-3 or a new one, if necessary, is matched against the proposed job or jobs, and usually against others in the promotional seniority area or "demotional seniority area"[5] concerned.

Placement Procedure in a Mutual System

Employees at Arvida Works who are no longer able to meet the physical demands of their jobs may be placed in any job

---

[5] A "demotional seniority area" consists of those jobs from which one employee may bump another with less seniority. There are 21 promotional and 6 demotional seniority areas in Arvida Works, the former being the more restricted.

openings in their own or other promotional seniority areas. However, they must be capable of fulfilling the requirements of the job to the level maintained by the average incumbent, without special training. They must also have more seniority than other candidates for the openings.

Efforts are made to arrange a transfer within the employee's own promotional seniority area. If the employee is unable to meet the physical demands of jobs in his own promotional seniority area, a transfer is usually sought within his demotional seniority area or, failing this, in some other one.

Wherever these placement efforts lead—whether to an opening within his own promotional, own demotional, or other demotional seniority area—one aim of a mutual system must be to avoid disadvantage to other employees. If a selective placement candidate does not need to be transferred at once, the placement section waits for a suitable opening. In urgent placement cases, when no opening occurs and it is necessary to displace another employee, this is done so that his move is to a job that compares favorably with his old one, and is acceptable to the employees. The move must really have his approval and consent.[6]

In instances when a physically impaired employee has to be moved into another demotional seniority area, the placement section tries to replace him with another employee from the receiving area who also has a physical impairment.

How do job openings come to the attention of the selective placement officer? Line management submits personnel requisitions to the employment department. The employment office advises the selective placement officer of opportunities that

[6] The operation of the system strictly on the basis of employee consent has been questioned from time to time by hourly paid and salaried employees. On one occasion a high official of the union at Arvida is reported to have requested during contract negotiations that physically impaired employees be given absolute bumping rights. The Arvida project committee considered similar proposals when it was hammering out the conceptual model of MSP. Employee consent was seen as a crucial element in a sound system. It was anticipated that employees would quite readily come to see the mutuality of their interests in solving aging-accident-illness problems. Experience since the founding period supports these views. The reader is referred specifically to Case No. 7 in the following chapter.

arise. First to be considered are the most urgent placement cases; the less pressing ones are reviewed next. When a candidate is found, efforts are also made to find a second prospective job, unless the employee's wishes and needs are fairly certain to be met by the first opening.

The interested line managers are contacted next, and an interview with the employee is arranged. The selective placement officer (S.P.O.) explains briefly in what ways the present job appears to be too demanding and suggests that a change be considered. No effort is made to hurry the employee into a decision. His opinion about jobs is sought, and existing possibilities are mentioned if he seems ready to consider them. If not, the interviewer may decide to postpone further discussion until the employee has had a chance to talk things over with his family or friends. The nature of the relationship between S.P.O. and worker is illustrated in the cases reported in Chapter IV.

Permanent and Temporary Transfers

When a physically impaired worker is permanently transferred to a job in another promotional or demotional seniority area, he loses his eligibility for a job in his old seniority area. However, he acquires seniority rights in his new promotional or demotional seniority area.

Should it appear that an employee with a physical impairment will recover the capacity to handle his old job, he is given a temporary transfer. He thus retains his right to the job to which he is permanently assigned. If he does not recover sufficiently in a year, he loses his right to it. Temporary placement under the collective labor agreement is illustrated in Case No. 7 in Chapter IV.

Convalescent Placement

In the fall of 1956, the placement of convalescent employees was explored by the employment office together with the safety department. Previous practice was to accept such employees as early in their convalescence as possible and return them to their old jobs, while allowing them to undertake less than the normal work load. This procedure provided the employee with an income and reduced the workmen's compensation rate, or the company's disability payments. The procedure, however, had certain unfortunate aspects. These reduced work assignments were difficult to administer and had unfavorable effects on employee relations. Under this old procedure also, some conflict tended to develop between the physicians, whose particular concern is the recovery of their employee-patients, and the safety department, whose work affects the compensation premium or the employee benefits department responsible for the payment of disability indemnity.

Under the new system, an employee reporting for work after a serious illness or accident is referred to the company physicians. If the physician finds him fit, the employee may resume his regular job immediately. If the examination indicates that the employee will probably be able to resume his regular occupation within a fairly definite period, he may be assigned to some full-time job, should one happen to be open which makes no physical demands exceeding the capacities indicated on his M-3. The employee then returns to his regular job as soon as a medical examination confirms his fitness for it. In providing temporary employment to convalescent employees, the company considers seniority and merit. If suitable temporary work is not available, the employee continues on the disability indemnity list, or recommendation is made that payments under the Quebec Workmen's Compensation Act be continued.

Company Physicians and the Employment Office

In the winter of 1954-55 when preparations were being made to install the new placement system on a limited basis, much thought was given to the possibility of an increase in placement requests. It was assumed that when it became generally known that new procedures were being developed, foremen and others would recognize the possibility of solving what previously were regarded as rather hopeless placement problems. It turned out that there was some increase in demands, but this was more than offset by the increased effectiveness of the work of the physicians and the selective placement officer.

One element in the success of the system was the support of the industrial physicians as they progressed from the first discussions of the system to its application in their work. The new system left existing medical services intact. The one significant change was that when an M-3 was called for, the physician was obliged to translate his medical diagnoses into judgments of physical capacity. The resultant success in placement added new meaning and value to his work and that of placement people. There was also an improved understanding of each other's roles. With this has come support for the physician in the maintenance of his professional code and relief from conflicts of authority.

Data for Research in Industrial Medicine and Placement

The first report on MSP[7] noted a rather high incidence of placement needs (20 per cent) for section chiefs in the reduction division of the Works. The report pointed out that this incidence was "higher than for any other employee category in the Works."[8] The following interpretation was offered:

> Promotion from section chief to foreman is a major step in a potman's work career. For this reason, section chiefs who have made their way up the exceptionally arduous promotion ladder, apparently feel compelled to conceal, even from themselves, any signs of physical impairment which could prejudice their chances. It is surmised that among the reasons for the high incidence . . . are: The nature of the promotion ladder; the related factor of age (the average is 42.7 years) and length of service; and physical requirements of the job, which include rather high environmental demands.[9]

This observation, duly noted in later work reorganization, could hardly have been made under the old system. Under MSP, with data on the placement needs and on the physical and en-

---

[7] E. Lapierre, E. Luchterhand and J. Pilote, *The Arvida Placement System* (Montreal: The Aluminum Company of Canada, 1957), mimeographed, 14 pages.

[8] *Ibid.*, pp. 9-10.

[9] *Ibid.*, p. 10.

vironmental demands of all jobs in all divisions of the Works, many useful comparisons are possible, and some are made routinely in the interest of improved placement.

Reorganization of the Janitor Service

In 1955, a major reorganization of the janitor service was undertaken at Arvida Works. As indicated above, on the mistaken belief that janitor work is light work, this work group over the years has been used expediently to place physically impaired employees. In the course of reorganization, 24 physically impaired employees in the janitor service were placed, either within or outside the janitor service on jobs which were better suited to their remaining physical capacities. These were difficult placements, requiring a total of 44 shifts of employees.

Light Work

In 1956, after some discussion, agreement was reached on setting up a light work unit, primarily for temporary placements. It was formed by bringing together some 12 to 15 jobs that had been scattered throughout the Works, and that often had been held by men with generally high physical capacity. The unit provided employment in some convalescent cases, and selective placements were occasionally made in it on a permanent basis.

In 1959, this unit was replaced by another for convalescent employees only, and was put under the supervision of the safety director. The work includes the repair and construction of safety equipment, repair of rubber boots and overcoats and the cutting of gaskets. The normal complement is eight men, but up to twelve have been accommodated. The average duration of convalescent assignments is 11 days. Besides facilitating early return to productive work, the unit was organized to aid employee readjustment to their regular jobs.

Changing the Job

During the analysis of the physical demands of jobs, changes were often recommended in the jobs themselves. For example, on one job the only reason a man of high physical capacity was required was that, as rarely as once a week, a 400-pound drum had to be upended. By reducing or shifting some infrequent but severe requirement, or by eliminating some particular hazard or condition, a job may easily be brought within the capacities of large numbers of otherwise disqualified employees. Such possible changes in jobs come to light in striking fashion when one studies them specifically in terms of physical demands.

Job Choice

Under the old procedure, jobs were found by persistent scouting. It was hoped these would fit the capacities and needs of physically impaired persons. The success of the old system depended on the good will which the placement person was able to develop among supervisors, and on luck. It was seldom that an employee was presented with a choice of jobs. As pointed out in the preceding chapter, choice was seen by the project committee as the best way to affirm confidence in the individual's capacities in his many roles.

Under the new system, it is usually possible to provide such a choice. One major reason for this is that all hourly paid jobs are listed in the master chart and because the physicians provide positive assessments of employees' existing capacities. As viewed under MSP, there are no one-arm or one-eye jobs and, in a strict sense, no handicapped people. There are only jobs with different demands and employees with different and changing capacities. Any one of the jobs in the master chart may productively fit some person who was once defined as handicapped.

4. The Workers and MSP: Placement Cases

> "Never mind, Jules, this is my affair.
> When I am ready, I will come to you."
> —Smelter worker to the plant
> selective placement officer

This chapter presents several cases, drawn from company files, which were dealt with by the selective placement officer (S.P.O.). They were chosen to illustrate the kinds of administrative situations involved in selective placement and the kinds of problems that confront the S.P.O.

This case material is prepared in two sections, designated "routine placements" and "placements involving problems of communication." The distinction turns on the initial readiness of the employee to change jobs. If the employee is willing, the placement is a relatively simple matter of finding a job according to his physical capabilities and then of making the necessary administrative transfer, or transfers if other employees are involved. On the other hand, if the employee opposes transfer, then the placement becomes more complicated and demanding of the S.P.O.'s talents.

The phrase "routine placement" is not used to de-emphasize the importance or difficulty of the placement problem. Nor is any claim being made that there exists a uniform set of problems; no two cases are exactly the same. A difficult case of long standing may involve considerable patience and tact, even though everyone concerned may desire the employee's transfer to productive work. Similarly, a case which involves seniority clauses in the collective labor agreement may be routine in the sense

71

of following prescribed courses of action and a willingness to
bring about the placement. However, it may be difficult if a
series of transfers are involved.[1]

Routine Placement

Case No. 1: *A Typical "Routine" Placement*

Adjutor Truchon, age 46, joined the company in 1935 as a
laborer. He served in the Canadian Armed Forces during the
war and returned to Arvida Works in November, 1945. He advanced to various jobs in the steam plant and was finally promoted to millwright. On two occasions, in 1953 and 1957, he
lost time due to illness, but in both instances returned to work
with undiminished capacities.

A reorganization took place in 1962, in which the millwright
group of the steam plant was incorporated into the larger group.
Because of this reorganization, Truchon was transferred to the
ore plant's maintenance group. Three years later, a third period
of lost time due to sickness occurred, following which the physical capacities report classified him as requiring selective placement. The report indicated that he would be incapacitated by
respiratory irritants and humidity.

The solution in this case proved to be quite simple: the S.P.O.
arranged a transfer to another maintenance group where these
environmental conditions did not occur but in which he was
able to work at his regular trade.

Case No. 2: *"A Young Accident Victim"*

Wilfred Lavoie, now 47 years old, was hired at the age of 19.
Two months after he started work, he sustained an injury which
necessitated amputation of his arm at the shoulder. The accident occurred while he was attempting to rectify the operation
of a welding machine. In leaning over it his arm was caught in
an automatic press.

Following an absence from work of nearly three and a half

[1] All names contained in this chapter are fictitious, with the exception
of Jules Pilote, the selective placement officer. Other information, such as
dates, ages of employees, is correct.

years, Lavoie resumed work with the company as a messenger and later as a weigher in the shipping department. This latter job involved special work arrangements, and a special apparatus was constructed to permit him to do the work. However, he declined the use of an artificial limb which had been provided for him. He held the job until 1957 when it was eliminated following a reorganization of work. He was then employed briefly as scrap and hard metal checker until October, 1958, when he was laid off due to lack of work.

Following a long period of negotiations between the S.P.O. and various department officials of the plant, Lavoie was rehired in May, 1959, as metal loader, but was again laid off in September, 1959, due to lack of work. There followed brief periods of temporary employment as helper in the caustic plant, janitor in the fluoride laboratory, terminating in layoff (September, 1960) because he was physically unable to do the work.

He was finally rehired in May, 1961, as addressograph and utility clerk. This was a permanent job at which he is still employed.

Case No. 3: *"Placement of a Long-Standing Case"*

Victor Gaudette, age 40, began working for the company in 1943 at the age of 17. He worked intermittently until September, 1945, but with no employment period long enough to acquire a record of service with the company.

Permanent employment began in July, 1946, involving a succession of jobs in the reduction and casting divisions until November, 1948. At that time he suffered fractures to his right arm and right leg which were judged officially as "permanent incapacity of 30%." Recovery time from this accident was eight months.

On his return to work, Victor found he was incapable of holding his former jobs, and after a year of work in the potrooms as laborer, he was given the job of janitor in 1950, a position which he held until June, 1956. At the inception of MSP, Victor was considered to be one of the obvious first candidates for special placement: he was only 27 years of age; he had suffered a serious loss in physical capacities; and he had been confined to the job of janitor which at that time was considered to be an indication of failure.

There then followed a series of temporary placements, arranged by the S.P.O., which were designed to provide him with more suitable employment and to raise his "fallen spirits." Beginning in June, 1956, he was placed successively on a number of jobs: laborer in the mechanical yard, chart changer in the instrument department, a return to laborer, and shift trades helper on a variety of crews and under a variety of work conditions. While working as trades helper in the forge shop, he became ill, diagnosed as a "depressive state." This was obviously a reactive depression brought on by his failure to obtain satisfactory employment, in spite of ten years of effort in doing so. He was absent from work due to illness for seven months, during which he was under psychiatric care.

On his return to work in September, 1960, he was reassigned to the forge shop where he worked for 20 days, then suffered a relapse of two months' duration. Since November, 1960, however, he has continued to work in the forge shop, without losing time because of sickness. In the intervening five years he worked his way up to various jobs in the forge shop, and in May, 1965, was promoted to the job of plate worker. At present his pay is $2.66 per hour, considerably more than is paid on his previous permanent job of janitor.

Case No. 4: "'Routine' Placement with Complications"

Jean-Paul Robitaille, age 44, joined the company in 1954 as laborer in the landscape department. With his limited schooling (grade VI education) he was hired on a seasonal basis in that department. He was laid off 14 times in the ten-year period from 1954 to 1964.

In addition to his limited formal qualifications, a medical examination made in 1961 indicated a low tolerance for exposure to wet weather, cold, sudden temperature change, humidity, respiratory irritants, and wet working quarters. These limitations seem to have been present at the time of hiring, but were not indicated in any of the records. Following the medical examination in 1961 he was considered a selective placement case and was subsequently transferred by the S.P.O. to a number of temporary jobs: section man on the plant railway, potliner, helper (potrooms), serviceman (casting), ingot cleaner.

In February, 1965, he was absent from work for the first time due to illness, for a period of six weeks. His condition was described as coronary insufficiency. In addition to environmental restrictions listed above, his physical profile was marked to indicate no capacity for running, climbing stairs, ramps or ladders, reclining, or working on cluttered floors. At that time, he was placed by S.P.O. in the job of laborer, power division. This is a permanent job within his physical capacities, and one which he is performing satisfactorily. This change from temporary to permanent employment job status might not have been possible without MSP and the efforts of its placement officer.

Case No. 5: *"Illness Victim"*

Mention will be made below (Chapter VI) that MSP operations have tended to reduce the periods of employee disability as measured by total disability payments. The employment history of August Desbiens serves to indicate how such reductions may come about. August is 44 years of age, with 11 years service with the company. A helper millwright in the mechanical division, he had an attack of bronchitis which kept him off work for four months in 1956, following which he returned to his former job. In 1957, he was off work for one month due to an attack of nephritis. At this point his case was taken up by the S.P.O., following which he was transferred to the job of hand burner in the mechanical division. He held that job until early 1958, when he was laid off because there was no work, and was rehired in July, 1958, as a serviceman (remelt) in the casting division. In August, 1958, he suffered a concussion, which kept him off work for three weeks, after which he returned to the casting division as machine pourer where he stayed until July, 1959. There followed an eleven-month absence caused by chronic infection of the pancreas, after which he was transferred by the S.P.O. to jobs of pot reconditioner, potliner, truck driver, carbon changer, then back to potliner and truck driver. These jobs all involved relatively low physical demands, during which time he was under close medical surveillance.

In January, 1965, August was found to be suffering from colitis, which kept him off work until July of the same year. On his return, he worked as laborer, shift helper in the acid plant, and in September, 1965, was promoted to the job of filtration operator, which he still holds.

By means of the placement system the S.P.O. was able to arrange repeatedly for suitable employment after variously disabling illnesses. Exposing this employee to several jobs after each recovery from long disabling illness permitted him and his supervisors to observe his capacities. The matching of physical demands and physical capacities guides the search involved in placement. Just when that search ends is finally determined by actual work on the job. In this case the S.P.O. had to arrange repeatedly with the employee and various supervisors for work periods on trial jobs.

Case No. 6: *"A Long-Standing Case Unsuccessfully Placed"*

Roland Francis began work in January, 1930, and in the course of his work career acquired 28 years service with the company. In his first years of employment he worked intermittently with short periods of unemployment due to resignations and layoffs. After World War II he became a regular employee.

In March, 1950, he was ill for 14 days with gastritis. This was the first of a long series of absences due to illness. In the next 15 years, there was only one period of absence due to lack of suitable work, but 14 periods due to sickness, which totaled 638 days. Of these periods, two lasted six months, the maximum time for which payment is made under the disability and indemnity plan. Besides gastritis, the illnesses recorded in his file include enteritis, duodenal ulcer and high blood pressure.

From the launching of MSP in 1955, Roland was virtually under continuous consideration by the S.P.O. He was successively placed on the jobs of potliner, gang leader, craneman, laborer, inspector of pots, cradle straightener, and concrete slabs straightener. In all instances, the placement was ended by illness. Although he has held his present job of concrete slabs straightener for about 18 months, Roland is still considered a placement case because of repeated absences due to illness.

This case is described here because it illustrates the frequent involvement of the S.P.O. in long-standing problems which are ostensibly caused or aggravated by factors extrinsic to the work situation. Roland was considered to be a chronic alcoholic. He was kept as an employee on compassionate grounds: he has been associated with the company for 36 years and had accumulated 28 years of service. Whether he would have been discharged if MSP were not operating is difficult to say. Much would depend on the interest shown in him by his superiors. But it is clear that the presence of the S.P.O. facilitated his transfer from job to job and keeping open the possibility of eventual rehabilitation. (It should be noted that the difficulties experienced with such cases have led to the establishment of a position in the personnel department called "employee counsellor." The employee counsellors—there are two at Arvida—work with employees who are known to be alcoholics and with their families.)

Case No. 7: *"Temporary Placement Under the Collective Labor Agreement"*

As noted elsewhere, MSP operates within the limits of the collective labor agreement. Under that agreement, seniority rules regulate transfer of employees, whether they are selective placement cases or not, with the following exceptions: An employee may be on temporary placement up to one year; after that, either he must be taken off the job, or the job must be declared permanent, and subject to occupancy by employees with greater seniority. Because of this "temporary" provision, it sometimes happens that a selective placement employee may be transferred by the S.P.O. to several jobs on a temporary basis before a permanent placement is arranged. A case in point is that of Edmour Duchaine, age 35, with 11 years of company service. In August, 1959, Edmour received a shoulder injury and was hospitalized for a brief period of time. The accident was noted on his record, but no lost time was reported. The injury involved a shoulder dislocation which affected his ability to raise his arms above shoulder height. At the time, this impairment was not considered serious enough to prevent him from working at his regular job. Following the injury he held a number of jobs until December, 1960, when he was laid off because there was no work.

Rehired in June, 1961, he went to the casting division as ingot cleaner, a job which did not require lifting materials above shoulder height. Later, after an illness lasting three months, he returned to his job of ingot cleaner. Two years later (October, 1963), his condition deteriorated to the point where he was considered a selective placement case, and was placed on the job of yard laborer.

In the following 2½ years, Edmour, with the guidance of the S.P.O., changed jobs 15 times. This period also included two layoffs due to lack of work and hospitalization lasting 3½ months for operations on his shoulder. All 15 job changes were made possible by absences from work of regular employees. Recently Edmour was permanently placed in one of the ore plants as sewing machine operator, which is within his physical capacities.

The number of moves made in this case is exceptionally high. A complicating factor in this case was that Edmour was reluctant to take a permanent hourly-paid position because he wanted a clerical position in the personnel department, a position for which he was not qualified. It took some time to convince him that such a transfer was impossible for him.

The frequent job changes in this case illustrate the value of the temporary work clause in the agreement, since it makes it possible to postpone a permanent placement until a suitable job is found. It also provides the S.P.O. with a pool of temporary selective placement employees to fill vacancies due to temporary absences of permanent employees.

In a somewhat different vein, but also involving the collective labor agreement, are the two cases of employees Louis Duchesne and Marcel Richard. Louis Duchesne, a heaterman in the ore plants, found himself in the position of being able to displace another employee who held the same job but had less seniority. This situation resulted from a reduction of operations. The junior man was a selective placement case. His displacement from the job would have meant being out of work, since he was incapable of holding any other job in the seniority area. In addition, he was a married man with a family. Louis Duchesne, a bachelor, elected not to displace this junior employee, but instead took a demotion with a loss of pay thus permitting the other man to keep his job.

Marcel Richard's impairment was such that he could only work at a job which permitted him to sit. On three separate occasions, Marcel was subject to displacement by other employees with more seniority. In all three cases, the employees accepted demotions to lower paid jobs, rather than displace Marcel.

Placement Involving Problems of Communication

Unlike the preceding cases, each of the following ones is presented in the form of a brief interview between the employee and the S.P.O., together with interpretive comments by him. The conversation as presented is not a full verbatim transcript but, rather, a foreshortened version, including all of the essential points in the interview on the basis of recall with the aid of notes.

Apart from making the placement process more realistic, this use of the interview format for presenting case material serves to emphasize the relationship between the S.P.O. and the employee as an essential part of the program. The S.P.O. talks to the employee, and by doing so, he attempts to achieve a better placement. Regardless of how much committee work has preceded or how many documents have been collected, the focus of daily work under MSP is the conversation between these two people.

What does the S.P.O., as interviewer, try to do? Good interviewing may be thought of in many ways, but one concept popularized in the mutual system of placement is *communication:* selective placement succeeds when the S.P.O. and the employee communicate effectively with each other. The S.P.O. has information from the medical doctor that the employee's health is being endangered in his present job. The employee may listen when the S.P.O. articulates this information, but will he accept what he has heard? Even if he trusts the doctor's competence to assess his physical capacities, will he think carefully about the matter? Will he weigh the seriousness of the hazards to which he is exposing himself?

The point of view in MSP is that communication occurs only when the employee recognizes a reduction in his capacities and is sufficiently concerned about their protection to consider changing his job. In this sense, there may be clear presentation of information but little or no communication. The employee may hear, but unless he understands what has been said, and considers changing jobs, no progress has been made. The S.P.O. has to know the difference between being listened to and being understood; he has to be sensitive to the many things that may block the transfer of meaning, i.e., communication. He must appreciate the fact that to the employee, the information that "I am incapacitated," may conflict with feelings, ideas and values such as: "I don't feel incapacitated," or "if I change jobs I'll lose pay, and I need the money," or "it can't be that serious." This dissonance, or discord, is much like that of the man who tries to save face by refusing to admit that he is getting old: "The doctor tells me I'm losing my strength, but I'll show him, even if it kills me!"

Seen in this light, the requirements of the interviewer in an MSP interview resemble those of a psychotherapist or a trainer in a human relations training group. He must be a good listener, patient about grasping what the interviewee is trying to say and why he hesitates to protect his health. This listening involves "what is being said" but also what the employee wants to, but cannot bring himself to say. The interviewer must also be competent regarding the organizational facts that bear on the placement situation—the possible effects of this or that decision on other employees and on department organization.

It is interesting to compare the selective placement interview as a method of communication with other methods, in which employees who are physically impaired are urged to take jobs which suit their capacities. There is a value system in our society which says that people should do things to protect their health and prolong their life as long as possible. Statements of moral and ethical principle incorporate this idea as guides to human conduct. Religious observances and economic, social, and political policies emphasize health and longevity as basic human rights. All of these become articulated and conveyed to the employee through the press, radio and television, as well as through company rules, regulations, statements of administrative practice, and clauses of the collective labor agreement. In spite of this "cultural blanket" of persuasive attempt, the employee may still consider face-saving and salary to be more important.

How may a placement interview under the mutual system lead to a different result? Probably by defining the problem as an individual one. The facts of the case are presented as an individual configuration of circumstances, not as some abstract principle or religious sermon. The facts are presented as fully and clearly as possible. And the choice is up to the individual. Not the company, not the union, not the S.P.O., but the man decides *what* to do.

Case No. 8: *Roger LeBeau*

Roger LeBeau was a section chief in the electrolysis division, 55 years of age with 26 years of service with the company. He came to see the S.P.O. at the employment office in 1958, following a long and serious illness.

First Interview

S.P.O.: "Roger, I see you're back from sick leave. You have been with the company a long time. Let's sit down together and have a look at your physical capacities, and see if we can find suitable work for you."

R.L.: "Well, you know I've always worked hard here. I think I deserve some consideration from the company. It's too dangerous for me to go back to my job—but I can't afford a loss of salary. I've lost enough money as it is."

S.P.O.: "Roger, just for the moment, let's have a look at your physical capacities form so we can understand what are your physical lim-

Reflections of the S.P.O.: This man presents a real problem. He is aggressive, and is still recovering from his illness. Proceed cautious-

itations. You can verify the comments which were made on the form, and the explanations made about your . . ."

ly. Try to be objective in explaining his physical profile to him. Otherwise his anxiety may prevent him from understanding what I have to say.

R.L.: "I know very well I can't go back to my old job. But I don't want to lose any income. The company owes me that."

S.P.O.: "Roger, while we're waiting to find a job to your liking, I'll send you to the rehabilitation department with old man Devost. The work is not too hard, and there you can get used to working again."

He no longer speaks of getting his old job back—so I have made my point. That is enough for now: he seems tired, his face is flushed, and he is starting to perspire. I will offer him the job in rehabilitation, and give him time to get over the shock of changing jobs.

R.L.: "Good idea—but find me a job as soon as possible."

After a period of several weeks in the rehabilitation department and a brief period of work as journeyman in the shops, Roger asked for time off for two weeks, saying he needed a rest. In the meantime, an opening as tool repairman became available. Following negotiations between the department authorities and the S.P.O., it was decided that future incumbents of that job would be required to work only on the day shift.

Second Interview

S.P.O.: "How is rehabilitation going, Roger?"

R.L.: "I like it very much, you should see me there" (with not too convincing a tone of voice). "Have you got something to offer me?"

S.P.O.: "I have a job of tool room attendant on day shift in the shack of 46" (workshop of pot line number 46).

R.L.: "What's the pay?"

S.P.O.: "$1.86."

R.L.: "That's not enough."

Reflection of the S.P.O.: He is ready for a change: he understands he needs a different job. During the time since the first interview he has become less anxious about his inability to go back to his old job. He has made his decision; he is receptive and open to my suggestions.

S.P.O.: "Well, you know, Roger, if you're on a job you can handle you earn more pay than even a foreman would if he was off sick and couldn't keep up with his work."

Roger accepted the job and worked for five years without absence due to illness.

Case No. 9: *Jean Bergeron*

Jean Bergeron, rod raiser in the electrolysis division, age 59, 25 years service, became a placement case following a regular medical examination made on January 4, 1956.

First Interview

S.P.O.: "Jean, you are getting on in years and you have given good work to the company. Since your medical examination the doctor finds that your capacities are diminished. This is the time . . ."

Reflections of the S.P.O.: I have begun badly—I should not have mentioned the word "diminished." I must find a way to establish rapport as soon as possible.

J.B.: "Wait a minute, there, I do my job, I am the best rod raiser on the line; look at this lump on my right side here—touch it, it is hard as wood."

S.P.O.: "Say, that is really something. How can you work when you have a tumor like that?"

J.B.: "My boss thinks I'm tough—he's satisfied with me; I don't get tired or anything. It takes a small old man like me to do the work. I like to kid the young men about it."

I have "communicated" by emphasizing that the man has a tumor. Since this is a serious situation, I will suggest a less dangerous job.

S.P.O.: "You like to play the 'old man.' Maybe you should take it a little easier. Don't you think it would be a good idea if I sent you to the tool room for a while?"

J.B.: "OK, I'll try it."

He seems to accept too quickly; he seems to realize the risk he is taking but he is probably not very

> convinced that he needs another
> job. He will want to continue to
> play the hero. All the same, I will
> transfer him and we'll see what
> happens.

Two and one half months passed and Jean returned to his old
job of rod raiser, vexed by the protestations of the S.P.O. According to his manager, "the old man does his job—a damn good
job in fact!" At this point in the development of MSP the manager was not completely convinced of the value of the system
and was still judging the man according to superficial impressions
about his physical capacities, rather than by medical information. The formal and informal organization were working somewhat at cross purposes.

In 1960, after the periodic medical examination of that date,
the S.P.O. offered the man a new tentative placement. (He had
succeeded in evading all medical examinations in the meantime.)

Second Interview

S.P.O.: "Jean, looking at your medical examination, it is more and
more apparent that you would
benefit by a job change."

J.B.: "I know, I know. The doctor
doesn't know what he's talking
about."

S.P.O.: "Jean, why don't you go to
see your family doctor?"

J.B.: "All right, I think that is a
good idea."

S.P.O.: "Jean, according to your
foreman, you are no longer producing what you used to. I would
like to have you try the job in
the tool room. If that does not
work out, you might try the job
of baker."

I have information (received by
telephone) about this man that he
is not doing his job. I have to be
firm about a transfer.

On February 2, 1960, Jean accepted the job of tool repairman,
but on February 8, 1960, he returned to his former job of rod
raiser. On February 14, 1960, he took the job of stud inserter.
On February 20, 1960, he was given a medical examination. On

February 27, 1960, he accepted the job of baker in the potrooms which he held until his retirement in November, 1962.

The point to be understood in this case is that the manager failed to acknowledge the fact that the employee apparently was no longer able to work at the level required on his job, and covered up for him. This led the worker to deny the soundness of the medical assessment and made the efforts of the S.P.O. ineffective. It took four years for the job change to occur, a delay which benefited no one, least of all the employee who was needlessly exposed to health hazards.

Case No. 10: *Georges Bazinet*

Georges Bazinet was an operator of a mud-thickening machine in ore plant number one. He became a placement case following several absences due to illness. One of the essential facts about the case was that although the man's foreman, superintendent, and manager of the division all agreed verbally that his performance was unsatisfactory, no one had the courage to put this in his records.

First Interview (December 1956)

S.P.O.: "Georges, your physical capacities profile shows that you have a health problem. Can I help you in finding another job?"

Reflections of the S.P.O.: The man looks frustrated, and it is a serious matter to him. I must try to put him at ease.

G.B.: "Sir, I have had a setback in pay. I was a foreman in 1944, and I was forced to give up my job. (All details were spelled out.) I want to be careful so it won't happen again."

It sounds as though he is not prepared to discuss a change of jobs.

S.P.O.: "Georges, let us look at this physical profile together. It indicates here that you cannot stand humidity."

G.B.: "That is true, but I arrange things with the other men working with me. They take up the 'sleeves' and it works out all right." (G.B. is referring to the fact that when a blockage occurs

in the reservoir on the edge of
the machine, the employee in cor-
recting the blockage is exposed
to humidity, heat, and some caus-
ticity in the air.)

S.P.O.: "Georges, if you were to
change jobs, would you be affected by a change in pay?"

G.B.: "My family has grown up . . ."
(The children are no longer dependent on him.)

Georges accepted a job change. Having done so, however, he
regretted the change, and asked the superintendent for his old
job back. The superintendent agreed and informed the S.P.O.
that it was necessary to give the employee his job. The superintendent failed to warn the employee about the risks he was
taking; the efforts of the S.P.O. were effectively weakened. Subsequent to the return to his old job, the employee was absent
from work repeatedly for the next several years, during which
time he received sickness indemnity payments. As in Case No. 8
above, the action of the supervisor served to cover up difficulties,
exposing the employee to health hazards and undermining the
work of the S.P.O.

As a result of changes in the job that were instituted in 1962,
the employee's performance reportedly became clearly unsatisfactory. At this stage, the case became one for the regular
supervisory staff and not for the S.P.O. Georges was assigned
as a relief helper. He then asked for a transfer to the sanitation
division as a janitor, and in June, 1963, his request was granted
after establishing his physical fitness for the job.

Case No. 11: *Phillippe LeBlanc*

Phillippe LeBlanc, section chief in the potroom, was 56 years
old and had 15 years of service when the MSP was set up. In
the preceding six years he had frequently been absent from work
due to illness. His case was brought up for selective placement
because of the lessening of his physical capacities. From the
employee's point of view, the problem was that any change in
jobs would probably involve a loss in pay.

First Interview

S.P.O.: "Phillippe, you know that my job is to deal with employees when they come back to work after being off sick. If men want to change jobs I arrange it for them. In your case what can I do to help you deal with your problem?"

P.L.: "Jules, you know me, if I need to change my job, I will tell you. Things are all right with me in the potrooms. I know everyone there; everyone knows me. I do my work. The company can't complain about my work. When I am no longer able to work I will come to see you; do not look for me. I will come to you. I'm not worried."

S.P.O.: "Phillippe, that is certainly your business; you want to go back to your job, that's fine with me."

P.L.: "I can do my work."

Reflections of the S.P.O.: I know this man is stubborn. From his physical profile it is clear that his capacities are below the physical demands of his job. But he is determined.

Phillippe held his job for two years. A serious relapse followed and his physical capacities deteriorated even further. The next interview occurred on his return to work.

Second Interview

P.L.: "Jules, I've had a heart operation. You know I was close to dying. I have given up . . ."

S.P.O.: "That was pretty serious . . . but now you look well."

P.L.: "The doctor told me the operation was successful and that I would be as well as before. But don't bother about getting me a different job. If I need you, I will come to see you, all right?"

S.P.O.: "That is unwise, Phillippe; you should not go back to your

In spite of his stubborn determination, I hope that this time I can place this employee and keep him from risking his health further.

I thought he would be convinced by now, but I was fooling myself. He wants to continue working in the potrooms.

job. Look here, look at your physical profile."

P.L.: "Never mind, Jules, this is my affair. When I am ready I will come to you."

The choice must be left to him. It will do no good to force the issue. He has done his work well in the past and I know he will continue to do the same. The placement system is operating because he knows a job is available and the decision is in his own hands. The motivation to stay on that job is stronger than his fear of what might happen to him. I will let him go to his job, but I will watch him closely for any sign of further deterioration.

The medical profiles obtained in 1959, 1960, and 1961 were scrutinized carefully. The 1962 profile revealed the inexorable decline in physical capacities. At that time the S.P.O. decided to go to talk with him at his work.

Third Interview

S.P.O.: "Well Phillippe, how are things going with the old tomato? It's pretty warm today."

The case is closed. He looks well and happy in his work. I will just talk with him as a friend.

P.L.: "I am fine as you can see."

S.P.O.: "How are you feeling?"

P.L.: "I feel fine, as you can see."

(This in fact was true: his eyes looked lively and alert; there was no sign of an old nervous tic, no trembling. But he looked his sixty hard years.)

Although Phillippe had not changed jobs, the case was successfully concluded. Having suffered a major medical disability, the man rallied to make a recovery while maintaining his job. His determination to prove himself capable of doing the work plus the S.P.O.'s respect for his own decision were undoubtedly crucial to the successful outcome. LeBlanc's remark traveled around the plant, and became the slogan for the S.P.O.: "Never mind, Jules, this is my affair. When I am ready I will come to you."

5. The Managers and MSP: Interviews

Our general concern in this and the next chapter is with the effects of the mutual system of placement (MSP) on relationships within the plant and on plant operations. While the next chapter presents statistical data, this one reports the opinions and attitudes regarding MSP of a small but important stratum of managers and others actively concerned with selective placement.

In planning this part of the study, the hoped-for ideal was to interview a probability sample of management personnel stratified by organization level. Besides the lack of a research staff to conduct the interviews, there were other problems. The foreman level of management had been thoroughly involved in the development of the system, inasmuch as foremen had to endorse the job analysis work sheets. In the process they committed themselves rather fully to the system. On the other hand, the superintendents, responsible for various divisions of the plant, were rather far removed from the working of the system. Attached to each of eight superintendents and two general superintendents, however, were staff assistants who were specifically responsible for matters affecting employees. While the staff assistants did not have supervisory responsibilities over the men, they were rather close to them and well situated to sense their feelings. It should also be noted that the staff assistant positions were approximately the same age as the MSP, and many of the incumbents were acquainted with the inception and development of MSP. For all of these reasons, it was decided to interview the staff assistants. The interview material reported here was gathered by one of the authors (D.S.), in July, 1963, with supplementary material by the other (E.L.).[1]

Of the ten staff assistants, eight were available for interviewing. Interviews were also conducted with one general superintendent, the two full-time company doctors, the president of the union of hourly paid employees and the selective placement officer (S.P.O.). Of this list of 13, nine at least classify as managers, and provide justification for the title of this chapter.

The interviews were designed primarily to obtain the respondent's description of MSP as it affected his work. In addition, questions were asked about employee reactions to MSP and about the feasibility and desirability of developing similar systems elsewhere. It should be emphasized that the main purpose of the interviews was to obtain the widest possible range of attitudes and opinions. No attempt is made in this chapter to provide a quantitative statement of attitudes and opinions.

Effects of MSP on Administrative Practices

As might be expected, adoption of the MSP had the effect of facilitating the transfer of employees with physical impairments. As a result, such employees more frequently performed work which was within the range of their normal capabilities. The extent of this placement activity is documented in the next chapter. But in addition to these direct effects, introduction of the MSP also influenced a wide variety of administrative practices. One of these was active efforts to identify and rehabilitate employees who required medical treatment. One example may be cited. One of the respondents mentioned the discovery of an employee who had been working for about two years with two hernias, one on each side. The employee was informed that he was running a serious risk of aggravating his condition and was persuaded to undergo medical treatment.

An important though undramatic change, attributed by our respondents to MSP, was the reduction by line managers of the physical demands of many jobs, as established by the industrial

---

[1] Informal interviews were conducted by one author (E.L.) with employees at all levels during many plant visits in the first six years.

engineering department. Among the jobs mentioned as high on the physical effort component were several which ranked with the highest paid jobs in the particular divisions. One result of this combination was that the workers on these jobs tended to be the older employees in those divisions, those less able to handle the parts of the jobs which were physically most demanding. After these anomalous situations were discovered, jobs were modified and new job analyses performed. In one department all jobs were reanalyzed, and the physical requirements distributed more equitably among them.

The administration of safety measures was also mentioned as affected by MSP since the detailed job analysis required by the system placed great emphasis on work hazards, from the standpoint both of environmental and physical limitations of the worker. The employee's physical capacities report (M-3) is routinely used in all cases of promotion, selection and transfer, since the prospective employee or transferee must meet the minimum physical requirements of the job before his application is considered. Finally, some respondents said that the introduction of MSP had raised plant efficiency by giving greater attention to employee health as a factor in work. Some felt that by better matching of physical capacities and job demands, and by earlier discovery of physical impairments, employees were less frequently off their jobs and in hospitals. These respondents stated that MSP provided a systematic and comprehensive method for doing what had always been common sense.

Some respondents pointed out that the problems of physically impaired employees had become matters of great concern to the union. For example, it was reported that in many selective placement cases the jobs offered to the employee involve loss of pay, of status, or both, and the resulting loss of self-esteem leads many employees to turn to their union leaders for advice. It was said that the union has increased its attention to problems of selective placement. According to several respondents, this has been indicated by the following: (1) some tendency, in dealings with management, to emphasize physical and environmental factors in job evaluation; (2) some advocacy of early retirement of older, physically impaired employees; and (3) some consideration of plant-wide rather than divisional seniority for MSP transferees. Respondents seemed to feel that the lack of consensus on these issues reflected the complexity of the problems which MSP was developed to handle.

Most respondents felt that the existence of the union tended to ensure the existence of choice in MSP. They said that if the selective placement officer were to coerce employees into accepting recommendations for transfer, the union would then be brought into the situation.

To sum up this part of the interview material, all of the staff assistants felt that MSP had an important bearing on administrative practices in one or another area. They pointed out that MSP is a system where none existed before; that it cuts across all aspects of administration for the simple reason that employee health is an important factor in plant operation, as it is in the employee's life. The staff assistants recalled with disfavor the old procedures of having employees return to their regular jobs on a reduced-work basis as early in their convalescence as possible. They consistently remarked on the negative effects of this practice on relations between employees. The MSP was seen as solving that long-standing problem.

Effects of MSP on Employee Morale

As indicated previously, the provision of choice was considered by the project committee to be one of the essential innovative elements in designing MSP. Respondents were asked whether choice was really available to employees or whether this was only a slogan or catch word of MSP.

With minor reservation, the respondents made it quite clear that choice is real. However, there were two kinds of reservations. First, choice is limited by the shortage of openings, and second, janitor jobs are still included among the choices that are commonly offered. Another respondent emphasized the shortage of openings, noting that a backlog of selective placement cases exists. Respondents generally pointed out that an employee transferred under MSP is permitted a one-year trial period in the new job, and that he may return to his former job within that period. This was seen by respondents as guaranteeing the existence of choice. One respondent, who gave qualified support to MSP, seemed to do so because a number of MSP transferees into his division chose to leave it and return to their former jobs.

There was high agreement that employees with physical impairments should not be forced to change jobs. Even though a transfer was often seen as being "for the man's own good," there was general agreement that coercion was undesirable. Putting pressure on such employees was seen as damaging to morale. Respondents felt that employees tended to accept the transfer wholeheartedly when they were given a choice. As an illustration of how coercion is avoided in such matters, one respondent took considerable pride in describing his involvement in a case that dragged on for five years before the transfer was made.

Regarding the acceptance of MSP by plant employees, opinions varied considerably. Some said they did not know how employees felt about the system. One said that it was difficult for employees to grasp fully the manner in which job and physical profiles are matched. He added that since the company does not publicize MSP as it does plant rules or the pension plan, it was to be expected that some employees would not understand the system. Besides, many young employees, who have never worked for any other employer, have no basis for comparison with practices elsewhere.

One respondent said that employees who have been transferred because of physical impairments tend to work less efficiently than others. He interpreted this to mean that they were dissatisfied with the system. Although there is some counter evidence to this view of the efficiency of selectively placed employees (see next chapter), their morale is apt to be adversely affected if they experience a loss of pay and status, as well as the other personal consequences of impairment, whatever its cause.

A contrasting view of the morale of employees placed through the efforts of the S.P.O. was offered by one of the plant physicians. He stated that he had received testimonials from employees who had been transferred under MSP as well as from employees' family physicians. The selective placement officer, who had more to do with MSP than anyone else in the Works, stated that in his opinion, employees understood the system and approved of it. Another respondent said that he had heard no "gripes" from employees. He regarded this as significant since it was not uncommon for employees to "sound off" about a wide variety of practices in the company. It was also noted that many employees choose the janitor service over other jobs because it is administered by the personnel department rather than by line supervisors, and because janitors often move around to various locations throughout the plant, adding variety to their work. Janitor jobs have also been modified and equipment supplied to make them less demanding physically. Janitors were said to be supervised less closely than are most other employees.

One fairly common remark by staff assistants and others about employee reactions was that one cannot expect complete acceptance of the system, nor is this necessary for its effective operation. The purposes of MSP are to maintain the health and employability of the workers and to prevent the aggravation of physical damage they may have sustained, regardless of cause. The point was made that there may be general support for this purpose, but when employees face decisions about their own transfers they are apt to feel anxious and may be critical of the alternatives before them. In the words of one respondent: "The workers don't like to take a new job if it means less pay, but when it's a question of their own health, deep down inside they agree with the system."

To sum up this section, the statements of our respondents about *present* employee reactions to MSP suggest a good fit to patterns of response in other examples of innovation. Much has been written about fear of innovation and resistance to it at the outset. This typical *initial* reaction seems to have been rather successfully averted in the case of MSP by the work of the project committee as described in Chapter II. But what sort of response may be expected to the innovation after it has become an integral part of the "stable" order of things? The observations of our respondents seem, on balance, to suggest quite general acceptance of MSP by the work force. This, of course, does not eliminate expressions of concern by individuals at the moment of their personal involvement in the process of selective placement. (Expressions of such concern were documented in the preceding chapter.) The interpretation of rather general employee acceptance will receive further support in the next chapter when attention is turned to the extent to which the project goal of grievance-free selective placement has been attained. All that can be said at this point in our discussion is that *present* reactions of employees to MSP suggest that we have here, in McLuhan's terms, a clear instance of "the imperceptibility of new environments, and that what is perceptible in typical human situations is the old environment."[2] The old environment consists of jobs in a giant industrial complex occupied by familiar people drawing pay at prescribed times and rates, and experiencing the ups and downs of life. The "new environment," originating in a sociologically conceived technology for solving the age-old problems of work for the physically impaired, is encased in and functionally integrated with the old environment, which thereby lowers the visibility of what is new.

Effects of MSP on the Practice of Industrial Medicine

Most respondents volunteered the opinion that the work of the medical staff had undergone marked changes since the installation of MSP. Physical examinations are given to all employees on the payroll. Although examinations were given in the past, the effect of MSP has been to streamline their administration, and to establish a rotation system which is followed closely. The frequency of re-examination depends upon the age of the employee: those who are 18 to 32 are seen every four years; those who are 33 to 44 every two years, and employees who are 45 or over are seen every year. For selected employees, special examinations are scheduled every six months.

There is no doubt that the increased attention to employee health and the preparation of M-3's has added to the importance of the medical service in plant operation. Whether an administrative problem involves transfer, promotion, selective placement,

[2] H. M. McLuhan, "Address at Vision 65," *The American Scholar*, Vol. 35, No. 2 (Spring, 1966), p. 199.

accident prevention or rehabilitation, the decision includes attention to the assessment by medical staff of the physical capacities of the employee.

Several respondents pointed out that the nature and scope of medical practice has in turn been affected by these administrative changes. Medical examinations are now performed more carefully than they were before, and their use under MSP reflects a preventive emphasis in employee health in place of narrow administrative concern with immediate employment purposes.[3] In the opinion of the two full-time physicians, both of whom have worked with MSP since its founding and have also served on the project committee, there has been an improvement in the health of employees at the plant as a result of MSP. They also pointed out that there has been a shift away from the notion of health as absence of disease to a more positive stress on optimal capacity for work and other activity. Thus, when asked to describe how the health of employees had improved, one of the doctors gave the following illustration: "Before the system was introduced, a work group of ten might have had only eight able-bodied men. The eight had to work especially hard to make up for the other two who were not able to keep up with them. This was unhealthy for all ten but especially for the two who could not keep up. Now under MSP everyone pulls his own weight and this has a beneficial effect upon everyone."

The physicians emphasized that since the launching of MSP, it has been much easier than previously to protect the confidentiality of diagnostic data. However, instances of abuse of privileged information were cited. Thus after noting the urinalysis of a job applicant, one of the physicians referred the man to his own physician. Coincidentally, a member of the employment department spoke to the man about his "diabetes." In fact, no such diagnosis had been made, since the urinalysis evidence might have been due to non-pathological factors.

MSP poses special problems for the physicians; the two on full

[3] It should be pointed out that this preventive emphasis did not begin with MSP. Under the direction of the chief medical officer of the company, fatigue studies have been carried out over an extended period in various plant areas.

time admitted difficulties in preparing M-3's. One stressed the number and complexity of judgments involved. The other made the same point but in a somewhat different way. His difficulty is also with the translation of diagnostic information into specified amounts (stated in time units) of different kinds of effort. This translation would be easier, he pointed out, if one could have personal knowledge of all the jobs. He indicated, however, that this is not part of the physician's role, but still he said, "if only I knew the job the man was doing, and the jobs he might be transferred to, then it would be easier to judge his capacities." One physician suggested that the plant doctors should be involved in the job analyses which are done periodically in order to keep the master chart up to date. It was noted that in the development phase of MSP frequent contact between job analysts and physicians occurred through their joint participation in the project committee. This was said to be mutually helpful.

The difficulties which confront the physicians are very real. Faced with the task of judging human capacity, it is understandable that he would like to make the problem less difficult by phrasing his assessment in more concrete terms: "Is *this* employee capable of performing *this* job without danger to himself?"

No one had a recommendation for solving this problem. Considering the apparent effectiveness of MSP generally, no changes were suggested. The point made by the physicians was that it is not easy to prepare physical capacities reports and that this will be one source of resistance by industrial physicians to the development of procedures, such as those of MSP, elsewhere.

Both full-time physicians emphasized that the doctor and the selective placement officer have different but complementary roles and that it does not work for the doctor to move into the area of placement. Both indicated that preparing M-3's is not and cannot be precision work; that in placement, judgments about physical capacity must be made by someone; that it is best to have physicians make them, however difficult they may be. By making these judgments in specific terms, the physician gives the placement officer information he can work with. Finally, it was noted by several respondents that by assuring choice to the worker, the man's own judgment comes into play, and this can serve as a protection against error. By going to see his family physician he has further assurance against error.

Is MSP Exportable?

In answering this question, the staff assistants usually spoke of various kinds of resistance to change. They said that workers may feel uncertain and anxious about something new, that they worry about the possible loss of pay and status and often express this by their reluctance to accept a plant physician's report, claiming that they know better than the doctor what is good for their health.

Within supervisory ranks, one of the main sources of resistance is concern that the supervisor's own department may be saddled with a disproportionately large share of the physically impaired. With regard to exporting MSP, getting supervisors to accept the provision of choice for employees in selective placement was seen as a difficult problem since it involved the unlearning of well-established habits of giving orders, or simply "deciding what is best" for employees.[4]

Respondents emphasized that the foreman is potentially the most important person in any effort to develop procedures such as those of MSP. It was felt by one respondent that the foreman, more than anyone else, would need assistance in such efforts.

---

[4] The nature of dilemmas in administering choice is clarified in the observations of a research team in New Haven, Connecticut, which included one of the authors (E. L.):

> To be effective, administrators have to have confidence in their own judgment, a confidence nurtured by making decisions. But to administer choice means to inhibit the impulse to decide. . . . The art of administering choice is to transfer something of administrative self-confidence to others, and to permit time to pass. It is often necessary to slow down the decision-making process so that the decider can interact with family members and non-family peers and pick up the maximum of cues needed for his decision.

This statement is quoted by Elmer Luchterhand, "Research and the Dilemmas in Developing Social Programs," in P. Lazarsfeld, W. Sewell, and H. Wilensky (eds.), *The Uses of Sociology* (New York: Basic Books, Inc., in press).

One other respondent suggested that health services in industry could be improved by training foremen to collaborate with the medical doctors in counseling employees about medical problems.

Who Administers MSP?

As indicated in Chapter II, MSP was developed by a project committee composed of individuals interested in problems of employees having physical impairments. The committee had no budget, so members worked as volunteers, adding project activities to their normal paid responsibilities. The only exception to this was the project director, who was on loan to the Works for "five or six months" during which he had no other assignment. While the functioning of the committee was approved in principle, no official expectations for its work were ever stated. This informal status continued through the planning and design stage and the initial work of job analysis. Only after making the first selective placements under MSP was one person designated as selective placement officer (S.P.O.) and released from his responsibilities as a safety inspector. In this capacity, he became a member of the employment office staff, reporting to the employment manager.

In the beginning, the S.P.O. was occupied mainly with placing employees with the most severe disabilities who had been improperly assigned to jobs, and in extending job analysis. This latter activity was continued sporadically as part of the search for jobs for employees with severe impairments. Later, the S.P.O. planned and helped finish the analysis of jobs and the master chart. Still later, the S.P.O., in consultation with the employment manager and others, developed the procedure for summarizing employee physical capacities based on M-3's and prepared *guiding* recommendations each month for departments and divisions on selective placement problems.

In this stage, much of the organizational initiative for the actual selective placement of employees was in the line organization. The staff assistant, at the direction of his superintendent arranged meetings of the foreman, the S.P.O., and any others concerned with the selective placement case(s) requiring im-

mediate attention. In the interviews, reference was made to the
S.P.O.'s function as partly that of watchdog. Various respondents
mentioned the S.P.O.'s efforts to prevent the waste of openings
suitable for selective placement of impaired employees by casual
and ill-advised transfers of employees.

As noted earlier in this chapter, our respondents generally saw
the foreman as the key person in selective placement, since he
is directly concerned with transfers into and out of his unit,
and since he is also the best informed about possible consequences of the transfer on all of the people affected. Ultimately,
the decision on whether to change jobs rests with the employee.
Since he has one year in which to return to his former job, it
might appear that in a sense it is he who presides over the system. Also, as we have seen, cases are known in which the employee has waited as long as five years before deciding to accept
a recommendation to transfer.

From our description of the initiative and decision-making
processes in selective placement of employees it might seem
that there is little exercise of authority by any one individual. On
simple reflection it becomes apparent that this "peculiarity" of
MSP is one that inheres in democratic arrangements, i.e., ones
that are based on the exercise of choice and consent.

While MSP is decentralist with respect to the individual exercise of authority, it is dependent on the amassing and interpretation centrally of a considerable amount of data on jobs and
the physical capacities of people. The interview with the S.P.O.
indicates that it is in this area that awareness of organization
and of the problems of decision-making are important. He indicated further that he found himself personally involved in
"pushing" the system and assuming major responsibility for its
operation. He felt that considerable initiative was required of
him in all stages of MSP, including the interviewing of employees, counseling of foremen, and persuading supervisors to
permit transfers to occur. In general, he found himself taking
administrative action which seemed to him to belong to others
with more administrative authority than he. In other words, he
felt that the "burden of MSP was on his shoulders," that it was

up to him to make the decision whenever an *ad hoc* committee failed to act—"whenever each person thought it was the other fellow's responsibility." The S.P.O. stressed the difficulties of resolving the conflicting demands of the various persons concerned. He likened his position to that of a juggler who has to keep a large number of balls in motion. By letting a single ball drop, the performance fails.

It was quite obvious from the S.P.O.'s remarks that it was also intensely exciting to occupy the one full-time position in an innovative program. Besides, this position permitted—at times seemed to require—a hero role. In this position it was he who "sensed" placement needs and who possessed the particular combination of knowledge, skills and enthusiasm to perform the juggling act and keep the program moving. But with this went vulnerability to criticism by the few who felt threatened by the changes represented by MSP, and to blame for the selective placements that did not quite work out either for the man or his supervisor. Since deep satisfaction and a certain frustration were combined in the same role performance, and since there was only one full-time position under MSP, it was rather natural for the S.P.O. to see himself as the "vedette," the leading player. He seemed to be confirmed in this by the fact that some criticism of MSP was focused on him. He said, "I am like a punching bag, with blows coming from all directions."

Just how accurate is the S.P.O.'s assessment of the role of a selective placement officer with a set of procedures such as those of MSP? Unfortunately there is no adequate way to answer this since we do not have the testimony of another S.P.O. confronted with a similar situation. However, our interviews suggest some overstatement of his difficulties as target of criticism. On the one hand, some staff assistants found fault with his work, while conceding to him success in his innovator role.

It is clear from the interviews that the S.P.O. possessed a set of qualities which facilitated success in selective placement. As a former safety inspector he had a detailed knowledge of the plant, the jobs, the environmental factors, as well as an acquaintance with medical routines and records. It may be suggested also that the occupational association of the safety inspectors with medical staff tends to reinforce their protective concern for the workers. To be selected for his job, and to grow in it, a safety inspector must have and must continue to develop ability to work with people; to persuade workers and supervisors to adopt safety measures, he must show understanding in his dealings with them. As various respondents summed it up, work experience as safety inspector is a good preparation for the responsibilities of an S.P.O.

It may be recalled from Chapters II and III that much effort of the project was devoted to broadening and deepening participation in the work of innovation. This approach was indicated in the way the project committee and the job analysis teams went about their work, in the involvement of the foremen, and in the active concern for the sentiments of the union membership. Besides the general gains for innovation from this approach, one of the special purposes behind it was to prevent any opponent of the nascent system from singling out an individual or group which could be defined as *the* agent of change in the situation. Interestingly, the S.P.O. felt that for just this reason a team of two S.P.O.'s might have been able to work more effectively.

While there was only one S.P.O., and not a team, there was teamwork of another kind to which the S.P.O. credited much of "the success of the system." This was the backing of his immediate superior, the employment manager. The latter's view was that "quality rather than quantity" was to be the aim of the system. Close cooperation between the two men in achieving quality in placement seems to have gone far in forestalling complaints and formal grievances.

But the chain of support did not end with the employment manager. The views of the personnel manager of Arvida Works clearly supported MSP (see his letter dated 22 November 1954 in Appendix III). And he in turn received the backing of the director of personnel at the head office in Montreal (see his letter dated 10 January 1958 in Appendix III).

Concluding Note on the Interviews

In reviewing the interviews as a whole, the most striking fact is the lack of any clear line of criticism of MSP. While this chapter draws its title from the preponderance of interviews with managers, it should be remembered that the two full-time physicians, the president of the union, and the S.P.O. were also included. In general, a humane concern for the problems of the physically impaired runs through the interviews.

Finally, it is of some interest to note that our respondents tended to project this humane concern outward from the plant to the surrounding community, and to see it as part of the liberalizing trends in Quebec Province.

6. The Plant and MSP: Statistical Analysis

The task of showing how much a social program reduces problems as intended is one that is rarely performed with complete success. The difficulties of evaluation research bedevil the massive social programs everywhere and are not likely to be overcome in the immediate future. The reasons for this can only be hinted at here.

Had members of the project committee been able to anticipate the present shape and dimensions of the mutual system of placement (MSP), some provision *might* have been made for a more thorough evaluation of it than this study supplies. What could have been done? Since the setting is a private corporation, should part of the worth of an effort such as MSP be sought in financial returns to investors? If so, how would one partial out the effects of MSP from those of innumerable other factors of a social and technical nature? That difficulty would have been aggravated by uncertainties about the nature and scope of the system being planned.

Then why not look at the supposedly salutary effects of MSP on the selectively placed employee? Or on the functioning of his family? Certainly a system which affirms a man's capacities at a crisis-time in his work career by making possible a choice of jobs has implications for mental health and family well-being. Again, the design problems would have been formidable, to say the least. In the problematical circumstances of the project committee, no one seriously considered the possibilities of such a study.

As mentioned earlier, the committee worked without a budget. The only member without other assignments was on loan to the Works for "five or six months." There was little prospect of a permanent staff. For all these reasons it would have been quite unrealistic to withhold action pending arrangements for a rigorous evaluation involving careful definition of goals, design of measures, selection of controls and the gathering of "time 1" data. The only thing that made sense was to invest the committee's energies, for the limited time available, in designing procedures to reduce the backlog of placement cases and to minimize future accumulations.

In planning this study it was apparent that the data would have to be teased out of various records, since there were no measuring instruments designed specifically to assess effects. In most instances the records used extended through 1963; however, those on lost-time accidents went through 1964.[1] The following are some of the questions to which answers were sought from such records:

1. How many placements were made?
2. What evidence is there that men continue to be employed who might have been discharged without MSP?
3. How has the number of urgent placement cases been affected by MSP?
4. How have disability indemnity claims and payments been affected by MSP?
5. What effect has MSP had on the janitor organization?
6. What is the present distribution of placement problems throughout the Works?
7. Has the accident rate changed?
8. How many grievances have been generated by selective placements under the mutual system?

The Decentralizing of MSP; Effects on Placement Records

In the last chapter the question was raised: Who administers MSP? To answer this it is helpful to look at four different periods of MSP:

[1] During a visit to Arvida Works by both authors in 1963, arrangements were made to obtain essential company records. To have updated this report with all the most recent figures since would have delayed it seriously, with little promise of gains for the analysis.

Period	Organization and Administration
1. The founding period beginning in September, 1954, and ending in May, 1955.	In this period, the question, Who administers? would have seemed absurd. The unanimous answer would have been: "The project committee."
2. The launching of MSP. This period begins with formal inauguration of the system in June, 1955, and ends with the completion of job analyses and the master chart for the entire Works in October, 1956.	In this period selective placement and job analyses proceeded under the firm direction of the selective placement officer (S.P.O.).
3. Centralized, stable operation of MSP. This period began in November, 1956, and ended in 1960 with the inauguration of monthly summary reports on placement problems to the major supervisory units throughout the Works.	In this period, the participation of staff assistants and others expanded slowly but steadily. Much of the organizational drive continued to be supplied by the S.P.O.
4. Decentralization and organic growth. This period began in 1961 and is still continuing.	Rapid assumption of responsibilities for selective placement on a routine basis by major supervisory units. Decline in record keeping and other functions of the S.P.O., except the interpretation of M-3's, maintenance of job analyses, and preparation of monthly reports to the supervisory units.

The question: Who administers MSP? could be asked in all seriousness by the end of 1960 and the beginning of 1961. At that time the stage was set for a decentralized, organic development of MSP within each of the main occupational groupings or supervisory units of the Works. Instead of the S.P.O. being watchdog for placement opportunities throughout the Works, division superintendents and department and section heads began to accept the obligations of selective placement as a routine matter.

By June, 1961, the selective placement efforts involving participation of the center had shrunk considerably, while those in the supervisory units grew, according to statements by the staff assistants and others. For the first five months of that year, the S.P.O.'s records dropped off about 50 per cent, as shown in

Table 6. Although systematic record keeping was not instituted among the supervisory units, central records were discontinued since they no longer reflected the facts of selective placement throughout the Works. This decentralizing shift shows up in striking fashion in the figures for 1961 in Table 6.

This shift of responsibility from the selective placement office to the supervisory units throughout the plant is a major event in the development of MSP, with consequences which merit research for the period where the present study leaves off, i.e., the end of 1963. While this development seems to be in harmony with the model of a placement system offered by the project committee and reported in Chapter II, just how the positive consequences compare with the negative ones is a problem for empirical study.

Selective Placements in the First Six Years of MSP

Table 6 shows that in the six years from the inception of MSP in June, 1955, to May, 1961, 2,521 placements were made with the active involvement of the S.P.O. and the employment office,

TABLE 6. *Number of Selective Placements, June 1955 to May 1961**

| Year | Unclassified Placements† | Classified Placements† | | | Total |
		Permanent	Temporary	Stopgap	
1955 (June-Dec.)	129				129
1956	366				366
1957	384				384
1958	138			356	494
1959		135	82	240	457
1960		124	161	262	547
1961 (Jan.-May)		26	39	79	144
Totals	1,017	285	282	937	2,521

* The explanation for this cutoff date is provided in the text.
† Prior to 1959, placement records did not distinguish permanent from temporary placements. In 1958, the effort to develop a classification scheme was begun by separating out stopgap placements, those arranged for employees whose convalescence from accidents or illness was predictably short, and recovery complete.

or 420 per year. The unclassified placements for the period June, 1955, through December, 1958, may be broken down by retrospective projection from the permanent, temporary and stopgap placements of the subsequent years. (In the case of placements classified as temporary or stopgap, the employee returns to his pre-impairment job.) This gives us the following breakdown for the six-year period, June, 1955 to May, 1961:

Permanent	Temporary	Stopgap	Total
624 (25%)	618 (24%)	1,279 (51%)	2,521

Since no usable criteria exist under MSP for separating permanent and temporary placement by nature of impairments, we get a total of 1,242 placements of workers with reductions of physical capacity of some severity. The remaining placements were those arranged for employees whose convalescence from accidents or illness was predictably short and recovery complete.

Physical Capacities of Employees

The data for this section were taken from the reports of the S.P.O. on the physical capacities of employees for the month of June, 1962 and 1963. The physical capacities code used in Table 7 is explained in the note supplied and also in Chapter III.

Persons classified under code 4 are selectively placed and are not to be displaced by their supervisors without consulting the employment office. Code 4 employees tend to have relatively severe impairments which, under the circumstances prevailing before MSP, would have made them unemployable in most instances. The few who might have been retained on compassionate grounds typically would have done their jobs on a reduced-work basis. It may be concluded, therefore, that one employee in 13 or 14 is able to hold down a job in the Works, fulfilling its normal requirements, as a result of MSP.

In this connection it is important to note in Table 7 that slightly more than half of the employees have the capacities to meet the full range of physical and environmental requirements of the jobs in the Works. The percentage of the work force classified under code 1 was 58 per cent in June, 1962, and 53 per cent

TABLE 7. *Summary of the Physical Capacities of Hourly Paid Employees, June 1962 and 1963*

Physical Capacities Code Number*	June, 1962		June 1963	
	Number	Per cent	Number	Per cent
1	2,424	58.10	2,150	53.03
2	145	3.48	193	4.76
3	603	14.45	973	24.00
4	337	8.08	292	7.20
5	663	15.89	446	11.01
Totals	4,172	100.00	4,054	100.00

* 1 = Full physical; full environmental; 2 = Limited physical; full environmental; 3 = Full physical; limited environmental; 4 = Selective placement case (not to be displaced without consulting employment office); 5 = Placement to be made (serious placement problem).

in 1963. This decline is congruent with the expected retention of employees with physical impairments by efficient selective placement, and is consistent with the trend toward an older work force.

The aging of the work force is indicated in Table 1, Chapter I, which shows the mean age of the hourly paid employees for four dates, selected to represent the employment peak for the year. According to that table, in the eight years between April, 1955, and May, 1963, the mean age increased from 36.4 to 44.3 years. Largely because of curtailment of production, the work force was reduced by some 3,000 between those dates. Under seniority rules, this reduction affected more workers in the lower age categories than in the older ones.

Another factor which may contribute slightly to the increase in mean age is the informal recognition by most people of the continued needs, and the capacity for service of society's older members. If MSP has affected the aging of the work force, it has done so by facilitating the continual productive integration of aging employees in the work force and conceivably by some slight prolongation of life.

It is significant that the percentage of employees classified as serious placement cases decreased from nearly 16 per cent in

1962 to 11 per cent in 1963 (see the figures for physical capacities code 5, in Table 7). In absolute terms, there were 217 fewer employees requiring selective placement in 1963 than in 1962, years when the size of the hourly payroll declined only slightly (from 4,174 to 4,054). It follows that, contrary to common belief, an increase in the mean age of employees need not always result in an increase in serious placement cases.

Data on Disability Indemnity Claims

From the records of disability indemnity claims data were obtained on the frequency of various categories of disease suffered by employees. Table 8 shows the number of claims, classified by disease categories, for the years 1954 and 1962. The data indicate a marked increase in diseases of the heart, blood vessels, the abdomen and digestive system—diseases which tend to be associated with advanced age. Decreases are to be noted in claims for diseases of the glandular system, and for non-industrial accidents.

Table 9 indicates that the *number* of disability indemnity claims

TABLE 8. *Disability Indemnity Claims by Medical Categories, 1954 and 1962*

	1954		1962	
Disease Category	No. of Claims	Per cent	No. of Claims	Per cent
Heart	17	3.12	40	8.28
Blood and blood vessels	23	4.22	38	7.86
Glandular system	38	6.97	6	1.24
Head, eye, ear, nose	59	10.83	41	8.48
Respiratory tract	81	14.86	75	15.52
Abdomen and digestive system	165	30.27	174	36.01
Genito-urinary tract	27	4.95	25	5.17
Muscles and vertebrae	20	3.67	25	5.17
Skin	46	8.44	22	4.55
Non-industrial accidents	69	12.66	37	7.65
Total	545	99.99	483	99.93
Average number of employees	6,204		4,171	

TABLE 9. *Number of Disability Indemnity Claims, 1950 to 1962, by Size of Work Force and Hours Worked*

Year	Number of Claims	Number of Hours Worked	Average Work Force	Claims per Hour Worked Times 10⁵	Claims per 100 employees
1950	486	11,306,656	4,752	4.3	10.2
1951	486	12,034,460	5,118	4.0	9.5
1952	445	12,196,388	5,763	3.7	7.7
1953	577	12,222,187	5,850	4.7	9.9
1954	545	12,929,270	6,204	4.2	8.8
1955	727	13,546,224	6,432	5.4	11.3
1956	728	13,307,403	6,332	5.5	11.5
1957	565	8,427,651	6,021	6.7	9.4
1958	613	11,005,828	5,346	5.6	11.5
1959	533	8,970,092	4,474	5.9	11.9
1960	593	10,722,684	4,254	5.5	13.9
1961	537	8,630,553	4,337	6.2	12.4
1962	483	8,212,720	4,171	5.9	11.6
Average, 1950 to 1954 (before MSP)				4.2	9.2
Average, 1955 to 1962				5.8	11.6

in relation to the number of employees and hours worked has been consistently higher since the launching of MSP than in the preceding years.

Two related explanations can be offered for the rather abrupt increase in the *number* of claims. The communication process in the course of the survey of the Works and the job analyses described in Chapter II probably influenced many employees to see a physician. Secondly, the new responsibility of the plant physicians to estimate employee physical capacities in specific terms probably resulted in somewhat better medical service. In sum, both the employee concern with physical fitness and the shift in plant medical practices probably resulted in an increase in the number of diseases found which required treatment.

It should be noted that the increase in the number of claims, however, was maintained over the eight-year period, 1955 to 1962. This is consistent with the aging of the work force and with the view that the number of employees showing a decline in physical capacities increased.

The evidence is fairly clear, however, that while the *number* of claims relative to number of employees and hours worked has been higher under MSP, there has been a decrease in the length of time such payments were required and thus in the actual amount of such payments. Evidence supporting this is presented in Table 10 which shows the payments made to individuals who were considered to be very difficult placement

TABLE 10. *Disability Indemnity Payments for 44 Hard-to-Place Employees, Placed as of June 30, 1961*

Case No.	Payments made during two years before placement	Payments made during two years after placement
1	$ 348.84	Nil
2	405.92	Nil
3	2,042.94	$ 403.08
4	1,871.04	52.32
5	767.11	Nil
6	725.49	Nil
7	2,096.40	183.30

TABLE 10.—*Continued*

Case No.	Payments made during two years before placement	Payments made during two years after placement
8	797.36	Nil
9	1,092.04	Nil
10	1,382.90	Nil
11	761.79	Nil
12	1,257.38	72.22
13	122.21	Nil
14	1,681.76	Nil
15	1,215.40	Nil
16	1,161.28	Nil
17	504.35	Nil
18	1,103.71	Nil
19	1,037.08	Nil
20	Nil	232.18
21	322.20	Nil
22	425.04	Nil
23	987.61	522.72
24	1,267.88	38.04
25	1,070.91	Nil
26	447.03	Nil
27	1,340.61	516.78
28	1,227.80	Nil
29	192.92	Nil
30	1,830.00	Nil
31	76.35	Nil
32	2,482.79	375.29
33	3,181.42	Nil
34	98.40	Nil
35	1,374.74	Nil
36	176.10	Nil
37	531.66	Nil
38	139.56	Nil
39	1,377.38	Nil
40	1,663.05	31.15
41	1,066.52	1,112.02
42	153.22	Nil
43	123.50	Nil
44	34.14	Nil
Total	$41,965.83	$3,539.10
Average payments	$953.75	$80.43

cases and had been placed as of June 30, 1961. Table 10 presents, for each case, the payments made for the two-year period prior to selective placement, as well as the two-year period after placement. For the group as a whole, the average payment was $953.75 for the two-year period before selective placement, and $80.43 in the two years afterward.

Distribution of Placements Throughout the Plant

Mention has been made of the fact that MSP has become an integral part of administrative procedures in all supervisory units and that it tends to be seen as a set of routines used in all aspects of placement. Data indicating the distribution of employees by physical capacities classifications in the Works are shown in Tables 11, 12 and 13. Table 11 shows, for each of seven occupational groupings in the Works, the number and percentage of employees in each of the five physical capacities categories. Tables 12 and 13 repeat the data for codes 4 and 5 respectively, but with the percentages based on the total number of employees in categories 4 and 5.

First of all, let us consider employees classified under code 4, those who are not to be transferred without consulting the employment office. Referring to Table 11, the percentage of code 4 employees among the seven groupings varied from 3.1 per cent to 69.4 per cent in 1962, and 2.3 per cent to 78.0 per cent in 1963. Although all groupings include some selectively placed employees, the sanitation section is comprised mainly of such employees; between 69 and 78 per cent of employees in that section were classified under code 4. This would tend to confirm the impression of respondents discussed in the previous chapter to the effect that "janitoring" is one of the regularly available choices for employees with physical impairments. However, it should be kept in mind that the section is the smallest of the seven groupings.

The data in Table 12 present a somewhat different picture. Here it may be seen that large numbers of code 4 employees are located in such important units as the reduction division, the casting and fabrication division, and the mechanical division. In

TABLE 11. Distribution of Hourly Paid Employees by Physical Capacities Code and Occupational Grouping, 1962 and 1963 (numbers in parentheses are percentages based on total number of employees in grouping)

June 1962

Occupational Grouping	PHYSICAL CAPACITIES CODE*					Total
	1	2	3	4	5	
Chemical	258 (66.2)	17 (4.4)	47 (12.0)	12 (3.1)	56 (14.4)	390
Reduction	777 (57.0)	54 (4.0)	168 (12.3)	53 (3.9)	312 (22.9)	1,364
Casting and Fabrication	472 (62.5)	26 (3.4)	137 (18.1)	40 (5.3)	80 (10.6)	755
Technical	47 (65.1)	2 (1.3)	24 (16.1)	17 (11.4)	9 (6.0)	99
Mechanical	632 (57.1)	36 (3.2)	171 (15.4)	99 (8.9)	169 (15.3)	1,107
Electrical	181 (63.3)	8 (2.8)	41 (14.3)	32 (11.2)	24 (8.4)	286
Sanitation	7 (5.8)	2 (1.6)	15 (12.4)	84 (69.4)	13 (10.1)	121
Total	2,374 (58.1)	145 (3.5)	603 (14.4)	337 (8.1)	663 (15.9)	4,122

June 1963

Occupational Grouping	PHYSICAL CAPACITIES CODE*					Total
	1	2	3	4	5	
Chemical	206 (59.2)	22 (6.3)	72 (20.7)	8 (2.3)	40 (11.5)	348
Reduction	643 (50.9)	74 (5.8)	319 (25.2)	49 (3.9)	179 (14.2)	1,264
Casting and Fabrication	409 (55.6)	30 (4.1)	206 (28.0)	24 (3.3)	66 (9.0)	735
Technical	109 (66.9)	7 (4.3)	36 (22.1)	6 (3.7)	5 (3.1)	163
Mechanical	620 (54.2)	50 (4.4)	270 (23.6)	78 (6.8)	126 (11.0)	1,144
Electrical	159 (57.4)	10 (3.6)	58 (20.9)	31 (11.2)	19 (6.9)	277
Sanitation	4 (3.2)	0	12 (9.8)	96 (78.0)	11 (8.9)	123
Total	2,150 (53.0)	193 (4.8)	973 (24.0)	292 (7.2)	446 (11.0)	4,054

* 1 = Full physical; full environmental; 2 = Limited physical; full environmental; 3 = Full physical; limited environmental; 4 = Selective placement case (not to be displaced without consulting employment office); 5 = Placement to be made (serious placement problem).

TABLE 12. *Distribution of Employees Classified under Physical Capacities Code 4,* by Occupational Grouping*

Occupational Grouping	1962		1963	
	Number	Per cent	Number	Per cent
Chemical	12	3.56	8	2.74
Reduction	53	15.73	49	16.78
Casting and fabrication	40	11.87	24	8.22
Technical	17	5.04	6	2.05
Mechanical	99	29.38	78	26.71
Electrical	32	9.50	31	10.62
Sanitation	84	24.93	96	32.88
Total	337	100.00	292	100.00

* Selective placement case (not to be displaced without consulting employment office).

the founding period there were marked tendencies to exclude from these units, and particularly from the mechanical division, employees with obvious physical impairments. At that time the janitor service stood more or less alone as a major concentration of such employees. This tended to further reduce the standing of employees in the janitor service.

TABLE 13. *Distribution of Employees Classified under Physical Capacities Code 5,* by Occupational Grouping*

Occupational Grouping	1962		1963	
	Number	Per cent	Number	Per cent
Chemical	56	8.4	40	9.0
Reduction	312	47.0	179	40.1
Casting and fabrication	80	12.1	66	14.8
Technical	9	1.4	5	1.1
Mechanical	169	25.5	126	28.2
Electrical	24	3.6	19	4.3
Sanitation	13	2.0	11	2.5
Total	663	100.00	446	100.00

* Placement to be made (serious placement problem).

The janitor service is now organized as a section of the safety department which, in turn, belongs to the personnel division of the Works. Earlier in this report it was noted that the janitor service went through a substantial reorganization in 1955. This has made it a greatly improved service in which there is substantial variation in the physical demands of jobs. Many of the cleaning operations have been mechanized. As noted in the interviews with employees in Chapter IV, it is not uncommon for employees to request assignment to the sanitation section.

A *formal* comparison of employee ages in the janitor service of 1954 with those of the sanitation section of 1963 suggests failure of this area of concern by the project committee. While 41 per cent of the janitors (see Table 14) in June, 1963, were over 60, only 20 per cent were over 60 in 1954, the fact is that the janitor service of 1954 is not closely comparable to the janitor organization in 1963. Besides the supervisory arrangements and the equipment changes, one of the most important changes is that members of the sanitation section, placed under MSP, are working on jobs within their physical capacities and have selected their jobs over other alternative offerings.

So much for the distribution of selective placements. What about the distribution of employees requiring such placement? Tables 11 and 13 provide this information. Table 11 shows that the distribution of code 5 employees among the seven groupings varies from a low of 6.0 per cent (in 1962) and 3.1 per cent (in 1963) for the technical division to a high of 22.9 and 14.2 per cent in the reduction division, i.e., the potrooms (see Appendix I). Since the potrooms had the highest percentage of code 5 employees, and the highest number of employees, its demands for selective placement services were the highest in the Works. Table 13 shows that 40 per cent of the need for such services in 1963 were in the reduction division. Clearly, the continuing demands on MSP are severe when, as indicated in Table 11, the physical capacities of 14 per cent (1963) of all potroom employees do not meet the requirements of their jobs, and 11 per cent (1963) of all employees in the Works are in need of selective placement.

TABLE 14. Age Distribution of Employees in Sanitation Section

Date		Total	20-29 Years	30-39 Years	40-49 Years	50-59 Years	Over 60 Years
April 1954	Number of employees	155	3	6	40	75	31
	Per cent of total	100	2	4	26	48	20
June 1963	Number of employees	123	0	4	13	56	50
	Per cent of total	100	0	3	11	46	41

Accidents

Information on the incidence and severity of employee accidents in the Works was obtained for each year from 1950 to 1964. These data are shown in Table 15. Figures for "lost time" were calculated as prescribed by the National Safety Council. Under the organization rules, a fatality is counted as 6,000 days of "lost time," and amputations are counted according to a schedule based on severity. It is clear from Table 15 that fatalities and amputations make up a large portion of the "lost time."

As indicated previously, the MSP was put into effect in 1955. The question is whether there has been a significant reduction in frequency and severity of accidents since that time. Because there is much variation from year to year in frequency and severity, the data are combined in three five-year intervals, shown as averages at the bottom of Table 15.

Table 15 indicates that there was an impressive reduction in both number and severity of accidents in the second five-year period (1955 to 1959) during MSP[2] as compared with the first period (1950 to 1954), before MSP. However, it is also apparent from Table 15 that for the third five-year period (1960 to 1964) there was a general increase. In the case of the category "others," the average time lost reaches a level which is higher than in the first period before MSP. This increase in "lost time" in the third period occurs even though there is no apparent change in the absolute number of accidents: in 1955 to 1959 the average was 54.4 accidents per year compared with 54.0 for 1960 to 1964. This suggests a tendency toward more serious accidents in more recent years.

In order to take account of variations in number of employees, a correction was introduced. Presumably, the greater the number of employees, the greater the number of accidents and the greater the time lost due to accidents. Table 16 was derived from Table 15 by dividing the totals for each year by the average number of employees for that year. In other words, the figures

---

[2] The mutual system was formally inaugurated on June 1, 1955, but the prior development work, including some selective placements under the system, might have affected plant situations.

TABLE 15. "Lost-Time Accidents"* for Hourly Paid Employees, 1950 to 1964

	Year	No. of Accidents	"Days Lost" Fatalities	"Days Lost" Amputations	"Days Lost" Others	Total "days lost"	Average no. of employees
Before MSP	1950	80	18,000	5,400	3,204	26,604	4,752
	1951	108	30,000	4,950	3,436	38,386	5,164
	1952	79	12,000	450	3,075	15,525	5,726
	1953	93	12,000	4,050	3,819	19,869	5,837
	1954	86	6,000	1,650	3,106	10,756	6,201
	1955	58	12,000	1,850	2,700	16,550	6,431
	1956	63	6,000	750	2,695	9,445	6,318
	1957	32	6,000	3,075	1,536	10,611	6,018
	1958	64	0	850	4,202	5,052	5,347
	1959	55	6,000	3,000	2,623	11,623	4,513
	1960	60	6,000	3,800	4,072	13,872	5,253
	1961	58	6,000	3,140	3,654	12,794	4,335
	1962	53	18,000	1,075	3,151	22,226	4,170
	1963	46	12,000	3,515	2,614	18,129	4,295
	1964	53	0	0	4,230	4,230	4,679
Averages							
	1950-54	89.2	15,600	3,300	3,328	22,228	5,536
	1955-59	54.4	6,000	1,905	2,751	10,656	5,725
	1960-64	54.0	8,400	2,306	3,544	14,250	4,546

* Figures for "lost time" were calculated as prescribed by the National Safety Council. Under the organization rules, a fatality is counted as 6,000 days of "lost time," and amputations are counted according to a schedule based on severity.

in Table 16 represent the average number of accidents, and average number of "days lost" per employee. This correction enhances the trend toward an increase in frequency and severity for the third time interval, 1960-64.

In sum, the data suggest that in the five years after the launching of MSP, there was a substantial reduction in the frequency and severity of accidents. In the third five-year period, however, a reverse trend, i.e., toward higher frequency and severity of accidents, set in. Since, under seniority rules, employees with low seniority are the first to go in a layoff, a reduction in the work force increases the proportion of aging employees, and,

TABLE 16. *"Lost-Time Accidents"** *for Hourly Paid Employees,
per Employee, 1950 to 1964*

Year	Accidents per employee	"Days lost" per employee			Total "days lost"
		Fatalities	Amputations	Others	
1950†	.0168	3.788	1.136	.674	5.598
1951†	.0209	5.809	.959	.665	7.433
1952†	.0138	2.096	.079	.537	2.711
1953†	.0159	2.056	.694	.654	3.404
1954†	.0139	.968	.266	.501	1.735
1955	.0090	1.866	.288	.420	2.573
1956	.0100	.950	.119	.427	1.495
1957	.0053	.997	.511	.255	1.763
1958	.0120	.000	.159	.786	.945
1959	.0122	1.329	.665	.581	2.575
1960	.0114	1.142	.723	.775	2.641
1961	.0134	1.384	.724	.843	2.951
1962	.0127	4.317	.258	.756	5.330
1963	.0107	2.794	.818	.609	4.221
1964	.0113	.000	.000	.904	.904
Averages					
1950-54	.0163	2.943	.627	.606	4.176
1955-59	.0097	1.028	.348	.494	1.870
1960-64	.0119	1.927	.505	.777	3.209

* Figures for "lost time" were calculated as prescribed by the National Safety Council. Under the organization rules, a fatality is counted as 6,000 days of "lost time," and amputations are counted according to a schedule based on severity.
† Before MSP.

if this interpretation is correct, leads to a somewhat higher accident rate. In order to assess this hypothesis, a correlation coefficient was calculated between (1) the average number of employees and (2) the average number of accidents, and also the average of "total 'days lost,'" per employee as shown in Table 16. It follows, then, that if age is a precipitating factor in accidents, there would be a negative correlation between the average number of employees and the average number of accidents; likewise, between the average number of employees and the average of "total 'days lost,'" as shown in Table 16.

The results were as expected from the above reasoning, but the correlation coefficients obtained were small and only one was statistically significant.[3] In other words, the trend toward greater accident proneness among aging employees is indicated by the data, although the trend is not sufficiently pronounced to be conclusive. The trend tends to be greater for the index of severity than for frequency.

What do these data on lost-time accidents say about the effects of MSP? Alone they give us no grounds to conclude that MSP had beneficial effects. Any number of other factors might account for the decline in the first five years, or for the upturn later. Changes in technology, safety programs, supervisory practices and other factors could affect the situation. A careful examination of these factors would be decidedly difficult and well beyond the scope of this inquiry. The point to be emphasized is that the results are at least consistent with the view that the introduction of MSP led to a more favorable accident record and not the reverse.

Placement Grievances under the Mutual System

Point 4 in the conceptual model of a placement system described in Chapter II states:

> The aim should be grievance-free placement. This should be made possible by:

[3] For the period of 15 years shown in Tables 15 and 16, the coefficients of correlation (Spearman rank correlation) were —.225 for average number of accidents, and —.479 for the average of total days lost. The latter correlation is statistically significant at a probability level greater than .05.

a. Offering employees a choice of jobs.

b. Insuring that an employee with an obvious physical impairment should not, on that account, be permitted to displace another with less service and who is physically fit, without that employee's consent. That is, the system should operate strictly on the basis of employee consent.

In order to find out to what extent this aspect of the model was realized, information was sought from the industrial relations staff regarding employee grievances. By averaging the experience of "typical" months during the first six years after the launching of MSP an estimate was obtained by staff members of 40 grievances per month. At this rate, the number of grievances of all kinds in the Works for the period from June, 1955 to May, 1961 would have totaled nearly 2,900. From the records of the S.P.O. and the industrial relations staff, only *six* grievances arose in that same period out of all of the employee moves required to complete 2,521 selective placements.

It should be noted that during this period the S.P.O. gave central direction to the placement efforts. He, and the employment manager to whom he reported, put much stress on "quality rather than quantity." It remains to be answered by further observation whether this enviable record of grievance-free placement will continue under the present, more decentralized operation of MSP.

Concluding Note

As described earlier, the origins of MSP were such that a program of evaluation research was hardly a matter for serious consideration. As the project began to assume importance, the problem arose of means to assess the impact of the system on life in the Works. Lacking well-designed measures, the authors turned to company records. The effort in this chapter has been to find at least partial answers in those records to eight rather general questions. (As noted at the beginning of the chapter we have had to omit consideration of the effects of MSP on the worker and his family.)

And what can be said about the answers to the eight questions raised? They are not without some ambiguity. If they were unambiguously favorable one might *feel* more strongly about the achievements of MSP, but such feelings would not constitute proof that MSP had been generally successful. Hard, conclusive research evidence for the success of a social program is exceedingly difficult to come by. One may believe that a selectively placed employee has been given a new lease on life and the prospects for his family greatly improved as a result of MSP. But can one *demonstrate* that he would not have been satisfactorily employed without MSP? One may have good grounds for such a belief, but what *evidence* can be produced? One may speculate about the mental-health returns of providing a severely injured man with a choice of jobs at a time when his physical capacities have been severely reduced—it is tempting to the program designer to indulge such impulses—but what can be proven? Belief is one thing and evidence quite another.

But if we reverse the argument—if we speculate that MSP failed to improve the situation in this or that respect—then the case for important accomplishments grows. In social programs it seems to be easier to disprove failure than to *prove* success.

Finally this chapter poses an interesting question: What are the implications of a situation in which one corporation breaks the norm of social disinterest in the placement of the physically impaired? This question recalls the problem of the well-meaning department head in the Works before MSP, who took "more than his share of the physically impaired" and then felt that his unit had been penalized by his socially responsible behavior. We leave the question for discussion in the final chapter.

7. Interpretation: Choice in Social Programs

Much has been done to prolong life and to protect or restore physical capacity. Although medical science has not eliminated disease, it has delayed the day when it becomes fatal. In industry, when we are resolute about reducing accidents, we do so. The success of these medical and safety efforts is facilitated by campaigns for public support. On the problems of selective placement of the physically impaired, much has been said and little done. No administration, public or private, however enlightened, is able seriously to reduce these problems without popular support and participation.

While adhering to concrete experience with the mutual system of placement (MSP), we abstract for discussion here those features which might inform the design of social programs. Although the achievements of MSP are limited to one company and a single problem complex, we regard MSP as a useful model of a social approach to social problems. Five areas are covered in this chapter. First, we review briefly the emergence of selective placement as a practical problem; second, we summarize the main returns from MSP and the difficulties with it; third, we look at the most serious discrepancies between the conceptual and working models of MSP; fourth, we attempt to explain why certain returns occurred despite those discrepancies; and fifth, we suggest further applications of the MSP approach to social problems.

Employee Definition of Placement Problems

For the victims of accident and illnesses, good selective placement is a major means to pass through crisis.[1] Among other

---

[1] Fred Davis, *Passage Through Crisis* (Indianapolis: The Bobbs-Merrill Co., Inc., 1963), especially pp. 138-141.

things, the crisis means loss of familiar routines; put in the language of white-collar workers, it means an upset in the career timetable. Specifically, it means lost income and usually an unwanted change of jobs, temporary or permanent. The upset means falling behind in important matters of living with perhaps no chance ever to catch up; "the normal timetable no longer applies to them except to show how much they have fallen by the wayside."[2] In still other terms, there is a feeling of lessened adequacy in major roles—husband, father, neighbor.

The aging are more apt to see good selective placement as a way of dealing successively with persisting problems of declining capacity. Work for the aging maintains familiar roles. It is the way one secures recognition from others—recognition as man, friend, and co-worker. The link of common employment has critical importance. Once this link is broken the retired individual loses his place among his still-employed friends; he is excluded.

Caretakers and the Physically Impaired

In writing about a neighborhood in Boston's inner city, Gans observes that "every society has what Erich Lindemann calls 'caretakers.'"[3] Gans uses the term to include people who give help and advice to others, and agencies and individuals that provide medical treatment, occupational counseling, financial assistance, training and other kinds of aid "to benefit the client, and who offer aid as an end in itself, rather than as a means to a more important end."[4]

Industry also has its caretakers. Workers who give advice to new men on the job, or help out when they fall behind are among those whom Gans would probably call *informal* caretakers; plant physicians, nurses, safety inspectors and industrial trainers are *formal* caretakers.[5] Besides being trained for their roles, the latter are employed as members of company staffs.

[2] Julius Roth, *Timetables* (Indianapolis: The Bobbs-Merrill Co., Inc., 1963), p. 105.

[3] Herbert Gans, *The Urban Villagers* (New York: The Free Press of Glencoe, 1962), p. 142.

[4] *Ibid.*

[5] *Loc. cit.*, pp. 144-145.

Their efforts to benefit their worker clients are typically performed within the framework of organization interests. Because of this complicating element in their caretaker roles, they are referred to here as *staff* caretakers, rather than formal caretakers.

Jobs vary in the extent to which they permit the exercise of informal caretaker functions. On some jobs an older worker who is physically unable to perform a demanding, but infrequent, task is able to get help from others. Elsewhere in the plant, such help may not be available. In most situations there are rather severe limits on the amount of "helping out" that is possible. A worker may not accept help which he really needs, lest he draw unwanted attention to his physical limitations.

A more common variety of informal caretaking is giving advice. Before MSP the inadequate nature of staff caretaking with regard to placement of aging-accident-illness cases made workers feel dependent on the advice of informal caretakers. In many instances, however, such advice was detrimental to the man in need of selective placement. The informal caretaker often had no more knowledge of placement possibilities or of the roles of staff caretakers than his fellow-work "client." Moreover, he was affected by the same belief systems and anxieties as his "client," who in any event was finally dependent on such help as the staff caretakers could provide with their inadequate procedures for selective placement.

In retrospect, the problem facing the project committee in 1954 was how to transform caretaking in the area of selective placement from an essentially bureaucratic function to a mutual undertaking involving as many employees as possible. It is this effort at transformation which the present study of MSP reviews.

Recognition of the Problem and the Decision to Act

Nisbet[6] writes of the complex processes out of which social problems emerge and of the historical currents that contribute to popular recognition of social problems. In Chapter I we referred

[6] See Robert A. Nisbet, "The Study of Social Problems," in Robert K. Merton and Robert A. Nisbet (eds.), *Contemporary Social Problems* (rev. ed., New York: Harcourt, Brace and World, 1966), pp. 1-24.

to wars and to changes in the factory system. We also examined the industry-community context of concern with selective placement at Arvida, Quebec. At this point we outline only the salient facts about problem recognition and the decision to act.

The triggering situation in the Works was dust on the desk of an executive. Annoyed that such a task as cleaning up should be done poorly, he discovered that others too had complaints about the janitor service. This led to a formal study of the service by the industrial engineering department. A serious discrepancy was found between the high physical demands of many janitor jobs and the management belief and intent that they should be comparatively light, and suitable for employees with physical impairments. A need for "adjustive activity," for some kind of corrective action, was recognized for this particular situation and for the more general one that gave rise to it.

Finally, there was a deep "awareness of ignorance." Neither management nor labor had been able to offer any worthwhile answers to the problems of meeting employee work needs properly in aging-accident-illness cases. Concern had been growing for a long time among managers and union leaders and the situation had been dramatized by numerous formal grievances. Various proposals had been submitted to rectify the situation, but all were rejected.

The experience with the janitor service had some important consequences. Circumstances had assembled, in this occupational grouping and to some extent in others, workers with physical impairments of varied origin. The project committee decided to treat the resulting needs for selective placement as a single problem complex; the placement of the aging was to be accomplished by the same basic procedures as those for accident and illness cases. It was felt that a worker who might react negatively to the transfer into his group of someone with a physiognomic defect probably would feel differently toward a normal-appearing person convalescing from a severe illness or an aging worker who could no longer handle his old job. A very young employee with little capacity to respond to problems of the aging might feel quite sympathetic to the placement problem of a peer who had a Saturday-night accident with his car.

Returns from MSP

Before attempting a final interpretation of MSP effects it may be useful to summarize what we see as the main returns from MSP:

1. In the first six years under MSP, over 1,200 Arvida employees having physical impairments of some severity were placed, half on a "permanent" basis within plant seniority areas and half of them temporarily. In the same period, MSP was used for nearly 1,300 stopgap placements, i.e., those for employees whose convalescence from accidents or illness was predictably short and recovery complete. In all, then, 2,521 placements were made under the system in six years.[7] While no records exist which would make accurate comparison possible, statements by knowledgeable members of management and of the union indicate that this figure exceeds by "many times" the selective placements for any period before MSP.

2. By dealing with physical impairments as everyone's problem, i.e., by hyphenating the problems of aging with those of accidents and illnesses, MSP made it possible to involve employees of all ages and subdivisions of the Works in the improvement of placement procedures and in their application. This involvement seems to have been one factor in the grievance-free operation of MSP in the first six years. (For all the personnel moves required to make over 2,500 placements, only *six* were the subject of formal grievances.)

3. Under MSP a vast amount of information about the physical demands of jobs was amassed and ordered for efficient use in selective placement. In the process of gathering this information, many jobs were modified to reduce their physical requirements.

[7] These figures are based on information in Table 6, Chapter VI. As noted there, prior to 1959, placements were recorded but were not classified as permanent, temporary and stopgap. To get such a breakdown of cases from the unclassified records, estimates were made by projection from the proportion of cases in the three categories for the years in which the cases were so classified. The two sets of figures were then combined to provide estimates of permanent, temporary and stopgap placements for the six-year period.

4. MSP facilitated the diffusion of greater job knowledge to managers in all areas of the Works and the discarding of some of the myths about jobs and handicaps. As the managers acquired experience with the system, they assumed more and more of the responsibilities for selective placement previously borne by the selective placement officer (S.P.O.).

5. Since the inauguration of MSP, provision for job choice for employees with physical impairments has been institutionalized, as indicated both by recent collective labor agreements and views of managers and union leaders.

6. Matching physical capacities to job demands is now standard practice in the employment department for all employees hired or transferred. This seems generally to have improved placements.

7. MSP has led to substantial improvements in the organization and quality of medical services; it has made it easier to protect the confidentiality of diagnostic information while increasing substantially the usable information supplied to placement personnel.

8. MSP has facilitated the early return to work of convalescing employees while minimizing the danger of physical setback through improper placement. This has involved organizing and reorganizing a light-work section in the Works in order to meet part of the need for stopgap placements.

9. As indicated in Chapter VI,[8] many employees have been productively placed who, under the circumstances prevailing before MSP, would have been unemployable.

10. The procedures of MSP provide highly useful information on the distribution of selective placement needs at any time, and the increase or decrease of those needs in the various subdivisions of the Works.

Various claims have been made about the beneficial effects of MSP besides those listed here. As noted in Chapter V, the full-time physicians claimed that employee health had improved under changes brought by MSP. Others have said that the increased attention to employee health has raised employee morale

[8] See the section entitled, "Physical Capacities of Employees."

and plant efficiency. Some have attributed to MSP the substantial decline in lost-time accidents, discussed in Chapter VI. Of those data we can only say that the introduction of MSP was followed by a more favorable accident record and not the reverse. We cannot assert that the decline was caused by the introduction of MSP. On employee health and morale and on plant efficiency we have no data which are adequate to sustain or refute claims of beneficial effects by MSP.

Difficulties in Operation of MSP

We turn now to difficulties encountered with MSP. The main ones may be summarized as follows:

1. The overwhelming majority of permanent and temporary placements at Arvida have been made on jobs at lower rates of pay than on pre-impairment jobs. Less than 10 per cent of all such placements have been on jobs at the same or higher rates. To understand this, two facts must be noted. First, the system operates strictly on the basis of employee consent and within the limits set by the seniority provisions of the collective labor agreement. Second, there have been substantial layoffs, and the plant has operated below capacity at various times since MSP was inaugurated.

2. Medical judgments about employees' physical capacities, when made by different physicians, tend to vary considerably. One of the reasons for this is the employment of physicians on an irregular basis to do examinations when the permanent staff is overloaded.

3. No efficient means exist to clarify the procedures and purposes of MSP to new employees with the thoroughness that this was done originally by the project committee and later by the S.P.O. Because of this, misunderstandings of MSP arise from time to time. A person newly assigned to an administrative post in the Works may view selective placement as a matter of the proper use of the paper forms described in Chapters II and III. Naiveté about the social character of the problems and their solutions appears in proposals to "cut corners" in

administering the system. Such proposals are usually based on misunderstanding of the depth of employee concern with placement problems. Such underestimation encourages the assumption of a benefactor role by placement people and supervisory personnel. Cutting corners is the specialty of a few who ask: "Why be a perfectionist? Why find three jobs for an accident case when an experienced placement officer should know which one is best?" And again, "Why spend time with the employee in analyzing the job? Instead of getting the foreman's O.K. after the job has been analyzed, why not see him in the beginning and finish the thing in half an hour?" And again, "Why all the explaining to the man on the job? It just interferes with production. And besides, things can be said better and clearer in the plant paper."

The Conceptual Model of MSP

It will be recalled that designing improved selective placement procedures became a central task of the project committee. In the course of its various undertakings the committee developed a conceptual model of a placement system which has been described in Chapter II. The elements of the model are summarized here for this interpretation of MSP. The new system was designed (1) to serve the needs of the aging as well as accident and illness victims, (2) to deal with abilities and not with disabilities of individual employees, (3) to use efficiently the generally high frequency of openings in a large plant for selective placement and to gather and maintain for this purpose data on the physical demands of jobs and the capacities of men. Further, the system was (4) designed to operate on a grievance-free basis by offering employees a choice of jobs and by insuring that all moves involved in selective placement are made with employee consent. It was planned that the system should (5) make possible early, safe assignment of convalescent employees to worth-while work, in part (6) by establishing a light-work section for stopgap placements and by discontinuing the practice of returning employees to their old jobs on the basis of a "reduced load." The new system was (7) to yield better medical records, permitting accurate projections of future placement needs by subdivisions of the Works, and (8) it was to begin when enough jobs had been analyzed to permit good distribution of selective placements throughout the Works. In each selective placement, the employee was (9) to be provided with a choice of jobs, and (10) to have one choice in the employee's old subdivision of the Works. In the design of the system, it was (11) intended that employees with permanent impairments were to be offered one or more jobs with pay at least equal to that of the previous job.

The inclusion of the needs of the aging as well as accident and illness victims gave the system importance for all ages. This was not a program for the select few, but for everyone. Complementing this was the involvement of all departments in the Works. This was to make the system organizationally equitable, improve the acceptance of administrative responsibility and open up placement possibilities previously left unused.

As designed by the project committee, the new selective placement procedures were to be based on a fairly precise knowledge of the physical capacities of people and, in time, of the demands of all jobs. It was intended that by supplying better information to staff caretakers, they would be able to discuss more concretely the problems faced by their "clients." Thus a better basis would exist for the employee to make his decision. He would still be free to deny the "facts" about the risks to his health in his job, but the prospects for reaching an early sound decision would be improved.

Discrepancies between the Conceptual and Working Models of MSP

The present evaluation provides some indication of a number of unplanned outcomes of MSP of a beneficial nature. Also, by the end of the first six years, the working model of MSP closely approximated the conceptual model on the first eight points listed in Chapter II and outlined in this one. We now discuss the three items remaining.

Item 10 states that:

> Whenever possible, the job choices should include one in the employee's own subdivision of the Works. This might serve the dual purposes of facilitating the employee's adjustment to the work group and, in accident cases, of raising the awareness of others around him to the need for safety precautions.

We have no data to indicate the extent to which such choices were found to be "possible." Without such data nothing more can be added to the earlier discussion of "lost-time" accidents.

In at least one area, that of grievance-free placement, the planned outcome was realized well beyond the expectations of the project designers. This achievement is interestingly linked with departures from the model on item 9 (the provision of a choice of jobs), and item 11 (that "one or more jobs should be found which are paid at rates that are at least equal to that of the previous job"). Both of these items concern the provision by the staff caretakers (S.P.O. and others) of adequate job choice.

Item 9 states:

> In selective placement, the provision of a choice of jobs would be the best way to affirm confidence in the individual's capacities and to buttress his image of self in his roles in the plant, in his family, and in the community. Offering a choice would be reassuring to the man during personal and family crises resulting from a disability. Such reassurance might actually reduce the handicapping effect of the impairment. Providing a choice might also contribute to the employee's acceptance of the job as the right one for him—one which he could do just as well as others who might lack his kind of physical limitations.

This item fails to set minimum standards for the provision of job choice, and we have no precise data on the frequency with which different numbers of jobs were offered to employees requiring selective placement. From incomplete records and interviews with the S.P.O. and others, it is apparent that in a high proportion of cases, a selectively placed employee had only his old job and one or at most two new ones from which to choose. (This leaves out of consideration cases in which there was a succession of temporary placements as in several of the cases reported in Chapter IV.)

Item 11 states:

> For employees with permanent impairments, one or more jobs should be found which are paid at rates that are at least equal to that of the previous job. While this may not be possible in some instances, there ought not to be a decrease in mean rates from old jobs to new. In job evaluation procedures, the relatively low weight assigned to working conditions and physical effort makes this feasible inasmuch as the impaired employee usually has skills which might be utilized to offset his disability.

It is important to recall that "less than ten per cent of all such selective placements have been on jobs at the same or higher rates (of pay)." How is it possible, then, that operation of the system has been grievance-free? In the speculations of the project committee it seemed critically important to employee adjustment that the pay after selective placement should be equal to or greater than before. This is not to say that committee members seriously expected that all special placement problems would be so happily resolved. However, the committee did feel that a loss in pay would lead quite directly to dissatisfaction and to formal grievances unless the employee found compensating advantages through ample job choices.

Choice as a Program Concept

Choice, as seen by the project committee, was a peculiarly potent program concept. Something of this sense of importance operated continually in the committee. The thing was to give back to an employee job choice—something he had tacitly surrendered to employers during his work life. The idea was to give this back to him as one means to help him pass through a crisis brought on by physical impairment. The committee was so zealous about this program element that it talked choice to job incumbents during job analysis, and largely built its model around it. In fact, the notion of consent by nonimpaired employees to the opening up of jobs for selective placement purposes was simply an extension of choice.

The emphasis on choice had tactical and strategic importance which, in this interpretation, kept the project from becoming an issue in the structured conflicts of labor and management. Along with other procedural planning, the emphasis on choice kept the innovation from running into trouble in a dozen different directions. It was proof of good intention; it was reassurance that job analysis was not job evaluation for pay purposes. The notion of choice disarmed opponents and rallied support. It was tactically and strategically one of the most important notions in the entire project. Yet, a casual reading of the selective placement officer's interviews with placement candidates might lead one to question somewhat the proper implementation of this project element.

The consequences of deliberate and planful use of choice in the administration of action programs merit careful statement. It will be remembered that the technical aspects of the placement system serve to make a vast amount of detailed job information available for selective placement work. With this centralization of knowledge of job demands, of personnel movement and of job openings, the bigness of the company can be turned to advantage in solving individual employee problems. This is technically possible because there is normally considerable movement of people within a large organization, perhaps enough to take care of the selective placement problems that arise. The hazard here is that with the concern for maximum use of placement opportunities and for technical efficiency in placement the employee may in fact be deprived of choice. To a considerable degree, the disparity regarding choice between the working and conceptual models reflects this tendency.

Dilemmas and Contradictions in Administering Choice

Perhaps an even greater danger arises in the inherent dilemmas and contradictions in the role of those who have to *ad-*

minister choice. To be effective, administrators have to have confidence in their own judgment, a confidence nurtured by making decisions. But to administer *choice* means to inhibit the impulse to decide and to make decisions quickly—to play the deity. The art of administering choice is to transfer something of administrative self-confidence to others, and to permit time to pass. It is often necessary to slow down the decision-making process so that the "decider" can interact with family members and nonfamily peers and pick up the maximum of cues needed for his decision. We suspect that the dilemmas of administering choice are a world-over problem. Wherever choice is important in the implementation of preventive and therapeutic social programs this problem is apt to arise. With all the emphasis on democratic form, the most "efficient" administrator often has an appalling adeptness for undermining democratic substance.

The answer to the dilemmas and contradictions in administering choice at Arvida was to induct blue-collar nonprofessionals into leading roles. This spared the MSP a certain amount of worker prejudice. It also made the placement process less threatening; the employee facing transfer felt more confident in resisting blue-collar pressure, if any, than the more subtle kind of the schooled administrator. The selective placement officer chosen to implement the mutual system grew into his role through active participation in all phases of the development work. In part, he was chosen because it seemed likely that contact with him in a placement interview would be as nonthreatening as possible. Thus the effort was made to eliminate subtle as well as gross influences that might be experienced as somehow coercive.

The Relevance of Dissonance Theory

Despite some limitations in the choice of work environments and jobs, freedom to choose was present in fact. In the matter of job choice, selective placement under MSP contrasts very favorably with previous procedures at Arvida, and with practice elsewhere.

As will be seen, MSP has turned out to be, in important respects, a massive and quite accidental application of the theory of cognitive dissonance which was first articulated in a book by Leon Festinger in 1957.[9] As we have seen, the "application" made at Arvida is not easily susceptible to rigorous test, but the rather startling record of some 2,500 placements with only six minor grievances calls for interpretation. A professional personnel group involved in that many employee transfers ordinarily would have needed a sizeable industrial relations staff to adjudicate a mountain of grievances. How then may "dissonance theory" apply?

In essence, dissonance theory serves to explain how people often come to favor, approve or even love things for which they may have experienced discomfort, displeasure or suffering. It is concerned with some kinds of attitude change that seem quite improbable. In relation to MSP, dissonance theory suggests that an employee, who *freely* chose a job which in particular respects was less palatable than another one offered to him, would find increasing merit in his decision. From the point of view of the organization, this might be reflected in a drop in absenteeism, lateness, and griping.

So far, this discussion of decision-making might seem to suggest nothing more than increasing commitment to one's own choice. The process of commitment, however, requires further examination:

1. The individual weighs the several advantages which inhere in the alternatives before him.
2. If he takes a job which appeals to him more than the other(s), his choice is consonant with his inclination and the situation remains fairly simple. However, he may be impelled to take a job with less appeal—a course of action involving emotional discomfort (dissonance).
3. Whether this decision was based on subtle or gross coercion, or whether it was freely made, he experiences dissonance.
4. If the decision was freely made, dissonance is progressively reduced by processes of cognitive adaptation.

[9] Leon Festinger, *A Theory of Cognitive Dissonance* (New York: Row, Peterson and Co., 1957).

5. According to Festinger and others,[10] the more free the choice of an unpleasant course the more favorably may the chooser come to regard that course in the future. Research findings indicate that subjects who volunteer for boring and generally unpleasant tasks develop more accepting attitudes toward them if the rewards are small than if they are great. Those who receive the greater reward for distasteful tasks see it as having coerced them into the decision to volunteer. Where there has been gross coercion or a substantial reward, the individual feels less personal responsibility for the decision made than if no strong incentives were present.

6. If the individual has grounds for tracing his decision to forces beyond his control, his action is less disturbing to him. Put in terms of the theory, he experiences less dissonance or emotional discomfort than a person whose decision, in a similar situation, cannot be rationalized by reference to external pressure. If the decision was freely made, the person cannot escape the fact that the choice was his own. And since he is not able to absolve himself from responsibility, he experiences more dissonance than the person whose decision resulted from outside pressure.

7. The normal individual attempts to reduce dissonance. While there are other ways, one common means is to make the cognition of the particular choice (the unwanted job) agree with his needs and wishes.

8. In general, the greater the information available to the individual about the rejected, but wished for, alternative (job), the greater the dissonance at time of decision, and the greater the attitude change in favor of the chosen alternative. Knowledge enlarges individual responsibility for decision by neutralizing or reducing some coercive pressures. In Arvida, one way of increasing information available to the prospective transferee was to slow down the decision-making process,

[10] Festinger, *op. cit.* Also see A. R. Cohen, "Attitudinal Consequences of Induced Discrepancies between Cognitions and Behavior," *Public Opinion Quarterly*, Vol. 24, pp. 297-318. Also see Cohen, *Attitude Change and Social Influence* (New York: Basic Books, Inc., 1964), pp. 73-80.

allowing time to pick up as many cues as possible about alternatives from other persons.

9. If in the implementation of MSP the hoped-for variety of job choices had been provided, maintaining the pre-impairment level of pay need not have seemed coercive in the event of a distasteful choice. Without ample choices, maintaining or raising the level of pay above that at the time of impairment might have been experienced as coercive, with the indicated consequences.

Discussion

Although many elements of the conceptual model were realized in the working model, the departures from the conceptual model were in areas regarded as important to the project design. In the operation of MSP there were important limitations on choice of working environments and jobs, and only about 10 per cent of employees placed under MSP were paid at rates equal to or above their previous rates. Why then did the working model work?

In the founding period, there was active monitoring by the project director of the placement procedure to prevent coercion by the selective presentation of facts about jobs and otherwise. The process of decision was deliberately slowed down in many instances in order to give time for employees to inquire about the new job(s) offered. For an employee to make the best use of clues about his job choices and the new situations of transfer, it helps if he has a repertoire of well-practiced social roles. The design of the project was intended to make good some deficiencies in role experience. By taking special pains with workers whose role experience and knowledge of the shop was meager, the chances of successful placements were substantially improved. The importance of listening for the expectations of the prospective transferee and how these might or might not be met was stressed in the meetings with the S.P.O. in the founding period.

On careful examination it seems clear that the insistent emphasis on choice—as a ruling project concept—resulted in the administration of choice in a manner essentially free of coercion. The planned safeguards against coercive influence in employee decision-making include the employment of blue-collar non-professionals to implement the program, delays in decision-making, some choice of jobs, and time to learn about alternatives. An *unwanted,* but effective, safeguard against employee *experience* of coercion was that pay on alternative jobs was usually lower than on the pre-impairment job.

In general, our review of the system leads us to conclude that in most respects it harmonized with the developmental needs of the employee. Chris Argyris[11] speaks of the need of the individual to move from passiveness to activeness; from a state of dependence, and little or no control over events, to "standing on his own two feet." He speaks further of the need to develop complex reaction patterns from simple ones; and to move from shallow and transitory interests and brief unconnected jobs to "long-term, coherent commitments." Further, the individual shifts from a short time-perspective to planning for and pushing into the future. The individual goes from a limited use of his abilities, through more demanding jobs or job-enlargement, to maximum use of his abilities and participation in leadership functions.[12]

The autonomy recovered by Arvida workmen through their involvement in a mutual system may not be very great. However inadequately, MSP does provide choice. It does involve ever-changing segments of the entire work force rather continuously in aging-accident-illness cases. By such means, there seems to have been some regaining of autonomy.

Finally, it should be remembered that this evaluation is based mainly on general company records through December, 1963, and on interviews up to and including July, 1963. The results of recent decentralization of responsibility for selective placement are not examined in this report and may well merit further study at a later time.

[11] Chris Argyris, "Being Human and Being Organized," *Trans-Action,* Vol. 1, No. 5 (July, 1964), pp. 3-6.
[12] *Ibid.*

Prospectus

The problems dealt with by MSP are common human problems. The program population consists of the hourly-paid employees of a large Canadian corporation. Without any grand intent originally, it now appears that some light may be thrown by MSP on other program efforts, including those of the "war on poverty."

One of the working notions behind this study is that success with one preventive or therapeutic social program probably has relevance for what may seem to be quite different problems. The idea that different problems are related by pervasive common elements is a logical extension of the concept of social systems and subsystems. The characteristics of people classified as aging differ from those of young victims of accidents or illness. Yet all may experience some loss of autonomy and feeling of powerlessness. So too may the school dropout when he attempts to fill adult roles in an automating society; and so may the Negro confronting discrimination outside the ghetto wall. In all these different problem areas, there may be such common elements as loss of autonomy and feelings of powerlessness. A program that succeeds in one area *may* have something to offer for programs in another, *if* the success bears on common problem elements. We believe that many of the problems associated with inner-city neighborhoods of our great metropolitan areas have common elements for which the program concept of choice is a crucial one. It may well be that few, if any, program concepts have greater relevance for reducing this cluster of contemporary social problems.

The assumption has been made throughout this study that extensions of the MSP approach are feasible. The term "conceptual model" implies as much. One extension of MSP—to Kitimat Works—has already been mentioned and suggests that MSP at Arvida is only one instance of a set of reproducible phenomena.

Margaret Mead points out that the dignity and treatment accorded to those with physical impairments serves well as "one

measure of the state of a culture."[13] She adds, however, that it
is necessary to consider the "level of technology and knowledge"
in making comparisons with other cultures, "for the difference
in the achieved position of the handicapped is so heavily dependent upon the state of invention."[14] We have noted in Chapter I the advances in therapy, training and other technical aids
to adjustment of those with physical impairments. The development of new drugs, surgical procedures, prosthetic aids and
specialized rehabilitation centers are well-publicized facts. It
would seem that our problems have less to do with the state
of technical inventions than with social ones. It is in this direction that we may have to turn if we would improve "the state
of [our] culture."

As we see it, the difficulty with most of the technical inventions and present social programs is that they take the industry-
community relationship as given. The approach projected here is
an extension of MSP to an entire industrial community. For this
shift from a company frame of reference we propose consideration of middle-size cities with populations ranging from 50,000 to
150,000. Present are the common human problems of placing people with physical and other kinds of impairments. Present are em-
ploying organizations which already, in some degree, share these
problems. Present are formal and informal caretakers, as defined
previously. We assume, as in Arvida Works, that the problems
and the resources for solving them are present in abundance,
even in greater abundance than in the Works. Additionally, we
may assume new community interest in concerting all manner
of social services in attacking problems that eventuate in poverty.

Three types of initiating centers might be considered: (1) a
prestigious company, so situated that it shapes opinion and practice in the industrial community; (2) a well-established community action agency with high standing in the industrial
community; or (3) a combination of both.

We invite attention here to the concluding paragraph of the

[13] Margaret Mead, "Creativity in Cross-cultural Perspective," in Harold
H. Anderson, (ed.), *Creativity and Its Cultivation* (New York: Harper &
Brothers, 1959), footnote, p. 222.
[14] *Ibid.*

previous chapter. The question was asked, "What are the implications of a situation in which one corporation breaks the norm of social disinterest in the placement of the physically impaired?" Some degree of participation by the whole industrial community at the outset might be important if secure advances were to be made in the employment situation of persons with one or another kind of impairment.

Whatever the nature of the initiating center, the new community system would require direction from a carefully constructed committee. Its functions might be roughly analogous to those of the project committee in Arvida Works. Only in one respect might help be needed in a middle-size city to bring to life such a program. This might be in locating and training one or more members of the directing team.

Appendices

APPENDIX I

The Nature of the Industry

The aluminum-producing raw material is called bauxite. Supplies of the ore for Arvida Works, Aluminum Company of Canada, are mined at British Guiana and Jamaica. It is shipped either in its unprocessed form or as a partially refined material called alumina. The unloading docks for bauxite and alumina are located at Port Alfred, 20 miles downstream from Arvida on the Saguenay River, from which it is transported to the plant by railroad. Extraction of aluminum oxide (alumina) from bauxite is carried out by the Bayer process. About four pounds of bauxite are processed to produce two pounds of calcined (dehydrated) alumina which in turn produces one pound of aluminum.

The Bayer reduction process involves digesting ground bauxite under pressure in a liquor containing caustic soda and sodium carbonate. The greater part of the alumina in the bauxite is dissolved in the form of sodium aluminate. The insoluble residue is removed by filtration and the liquor containing the dissolved sodium aluminate is transferred to the precipitation process, where it is reduced in temperature by heat exchangers and charged to large precipitation tanks. When a "seed" of fine hydrated alumina is added, precipitation takes place. Quantity and fineness of the seed, and the temperature and liquor composition, are controlled to give a product of uniform particle size distribution. The precipitate (aluminum hydrate) is separated from the "spent liquor" by settling, and fractionated; the coarser part

145

is removed and washed as the primary product, the finer part being returned to the process as seed.

The precipitated alumina hydrate contains nearly 35 per cent combined water which must be removed before the alumina is suitable for reduction. This dehydration is carried out in oil-fired rotary kilns which are approximately 260 feet long and operate at a temperature of about 2100° F. After calcining, the alumina is charged into standard-gauge hopper boxcars and transported to the reduction plants.

The reduction of alumina to aluminum is achieved in an electrolytic cell called a "pot." Electric power is fed to these pots or reduction cells in groups of about 130 in series. Such a group of pots operating on one electric circuit is called a "pot line." A typical pot line will operate at 45,000 to 50,000 amperes, at a total voltage of about 700 volts.

Alumina received from the ore plants (Bayer reduction process, described above) is unloaded by track hopper and overhead conveyor and distributed by cranes to bins above each reduction cell. The alumina is then charged to the reduction cell as required, by a valve arrangement on the individual bins. The alumina is therefore handled entirely by mechanical means from the calcination process direct to the reduction cell.

The reduction cell consists of a steel shell lined with a carbon hearth which serves as the cathode (the negative pole of the cell). Heat insulating material (brick or alumina) is placed between the steel shell and the carbon lining. In the cell, anodes (positive poles of the cell) are suspended from a steel superstructure frame, electrically insulated from the cathode. The inside of the cell is charged with cryolite, which in the molten state is an electrolyte or current-carrying substance. This electrolyte is maintained in the molten state in the reduction cell by the passage of electric current. The temperature in the cell is about 970° C. The basic reduction process involves dissolving alumina in the cryolite and decomposing it by the electric current. The aluminum appears molten at the cathode and the oxygen at the anode, where it reacts with the carbon and passes off to the atmosphere as carbon oxides. The aluminum, being heavier than the cryolite, accumulates at the bottom of the cell, from which it is tapped at intervals (about 1500 pounds every two days).

The operation of aluminum reduction cells is necessarily continuous and the tapping of aluminum is carried out on all shifts. In order that metal from the reduction cell may be classified and blended to give the alloys of aluminum required for current orders, samples are taken of all metal before tapping, the samples being analyzed spectrographically for common impurities. The metal is then selected and blended in holding furnaces in which it is held for a short time before being cast into ingots. Since the ingot is the final form in which metal is shipped from the plant, samples are taken at the final casting for spectrographic analysis. Purity of the metal so produced will exceed 99.5 per cent pure aluminum on the average, with a maximum of about 99.9 per cent.

In addition to commercial purity aluminum, alloys are produced by the addition of alloying elements, such as iron, copper, magnesium, manganese, titanium, chromium, zinc, lead, bismuth and silicon. Aluminum alloys are prepared in oil-fired furnaces, in batches of up to 100,000 pounds, by the carefully controlled addition of hardeners to the parent metal. Some of the hardeners, which are themselves alloys, are prepared directly in the reduction pots. Most of the metal is shipped from the plant in ingot form for fabrication elsewhere, but a substantial amount goes to the rod rolling mill in Arvida Works.

Analyzing the Job: A Reference Manual[1]

Analyze the Present Job

Each job should be analyzed exactly as it exists, not as it should exist, or has existed in the past. If the analyst discovers ways to make the job less demanding physically, or less hazardous, he should write his suggestions on the back of the work sheet.

Record Requirements Only

The analysis should include only those activities which are actually required by the job. Of all the things the analyst has to learn, this is one of the most difficult. For each factor on the work sheet, the analyst must ask himself: "Is this a necessary element of this job?" For various individual and departmental reasons, jobs are often made to appear more difficult than they are. For instance:

> A worker may climb down a ladder, or jump from a platform rather than use a nearby ramp or steps. Neither climbing nor jumping is a requirement since use of the ramp or steps would eliminate climbing or jumping.

[1] Instructions for job analysts have been revised several times since 1954. The changes have been editorial rather than substantive. Some of the definitions of job factors are essentially the same as when they were first developed during World War II, and reported by Clark D. Bridges, *Job Placement of the Physically Handicapped* (New York: McGraw-Hill Book Company, Inc., 1946). This manual quotes extensively from *Physical Abilities to Fit the Job* (Boston: American Mutual Liability Insurance Company, 1956), Ch. XII, which updates Bridges' treatment. The material presented here was selected and arranged for *reference* use by job analysts who have had some training. It is included as an appendix for illustrative purposes. An adequate set of *training* materials would include a description of the procedures used by physicians and by placement officers, as well as examples of the analysis of complex jobs.

"An arc welder may use his sense of hearing to help him maintain the proper arc by listening to the hissing sound of the arc. . . . Yet the job does not *require* the arc welder to hear. The important requirement is sight, through which he judges whether or not he is maintaining the proper arc by observing the welding process. Had the analyst listed hearing as a requirement, he would automatically have eliminated deaf workers from becoming arc welders, a job at which deaf persons work very well."[2]

A worker may stand at a bench while working rather than use the seat provided for him. Standing cannot be called a requirement of the job. Neither is sitting a requirement, since the worker may stand if he chooses. Sitting and standing are both optional.

Total Job

"The analyst should make certain that he covers the full range of activities required by the job. Some jobs may require a daily change in the worker's activities for several consecutive days. Other jobs may require a change every few days over a period of several weeks. In all cases the analyst should record the demands of the total job."[3]

Location Variations

"When the physical demands of a job are significantly different in various departments or even within the same department, the analyst should prepare separate work sheets for each different pattern of demands. When, however, the demands of the job are the same in different locations, one work sheet is sufficient, and the different departments in which the demands are the same should then be stated on the one work sheet under *Job Location*."[4]

Shift Variations

"The job should be analyzed for all shifts. If the demands are the same on all shifts, only one work sheet is used, on which the different shift numbers or names are recorded. Sometimes, however, significant differences appear which require the prep-

[2] *Physical Abilities to Fit the Job* (Boston: American Mutual Liability Insurance Company, 1956), p. 93.
[3] *Ibid.*, pp. 93-94.
[4] *Ibid.*, pp. 94-95.

aration of separate work sheets for the job according to shifts.
. . . On the other hand, if the workers on the job being studied
are rotated and the job requires them to work on all shifts at
various times, only one work sheet should be prepared to represent the *composite demands* of the job for all shifts."[5]

Special Assignments

"The analyst should guard against recording physical activities which are part of a special assignment and are not actually
required by the job itself."[6] For instance, additional physical
activities may be required when a worker is temporarily assigned the duties of repairing his own equipment which is ordinarily repaired by another worker. These temporary activities
should not be included in the demands of the job.

Identifying Information on the Work Sheet

The analyst should record the job title, the name of the de-
partment(s), shop(s), building number(s), place(s) where the
job is found in the plant. "One job, for example, may be located
in five different departments of the same plant. If the demands
of this job are the same in all departments, then only one work
sheet is prepared and the five departments where the job is
located appear on this one work sheet. If the demands of this
one job are different in each department, then five separate work
sheets should be prepared, one for each department."[7]

Recording the Demands of the Physical and Environmental Factors

"The boxes before each of the factors on the work sheet, except
for the sensory factors numbered 42 to 47, are to be filled in by
the analyst with the *maximum* number of hours each factor is
found to be *required* by the job during the work day. Sometimes
a factor may be required for less than an hour, and hence
fractions of an hour are recorded. For practical reasons, however,
the smallest fraction used is ¼ of an hour, even though the factor
may be required for less than 15 minutes. The next largest frac-

[5] *Ibid.*, p. 95.
[6] *Loc. cit.*
[7] *Ibid.*, p. 97.

tion used is ½ hour, and then occasionally ¾ of an hour. There-after the whole numbers from 1 to 8 hours (or however long the shift may be) are used. . . . The analyst . . . could be more accurate than this, but it is not necessary since the physician cannot be more accurate in stating workers' capacities and uses whole numbers mostly, using ¼ or ½ hour only occasionally. . . . The analyst should make sure, however, that he records the *maximum* number of hours each factor is required, for a worker must have the ability to meet maximum demands even though the maximum demands may not be required by the job every day. . . .

"The boxes before all factors which are not found to be re-quired by the job are to be filled in by the analyst with a dash (−) to show that the factors have been considered but are not required. . . .

"When required by the job, the other sensory factors (44 to 47) are to be filled in with a plus sign (+), meaning required. A plus sign rather than hours is used here since the time element is of little consequence. For example, the fact that a job requires color vision is important, but whether the worker must recog-nize color for several hours or only once a day is relatively unimportant.

"Besides hours, a few of the environmental factors call for additional information. In connection with temperature (53 and 54), the degrees of hot or cold are to be entered. For radiant energy (67), the kind is to be stated. Also, the kind of toxic conditions (70) found is to be named."[8]

Meaning and Use of R, L, and E

"R means right, L left, and E means either right or left, and apply to the use of either or both: sets of fingers, hands, arms, legs. The analyst uses R, L, and E in connection with the factors of fingering, handling, reaching, throwing, and treading.

"For each of these activities, a separate box appears for R and L, but no box appears for E. When an activity may be performed by either the right or left hand, for example, the entry for E under handling is made in the same box with R, and with an E written in after the entry."[9]

[8] *Ibid.*, pp. 98-100.
[9] *Ibid.*, p. 100. For useful illustrative tables, the reader is referred to the work cited.

Time Requirements

"Many jobs are quite standardized and their demands are more or less stable, varying little from day to day. Other jobs fluctuate, however, and often have wide variations in their demands from time to time. In all cases, of course, the analyst must record the maximum demands of the jobs however stable or however widely it may fluctuate."[10]

Definitions of the Physical and Environmental Factors

Lifting (Factor numbers 1-6) "Raising or lowering an object from one level to another by using muscular strength, usually by grasping the object with the hand or hands.

Carrying (7-12) "Transporting an object by using muscular strength, usually by holding it in the hand(s) and arm(s)."[11]

In determining the amount of time for lifting and carrying, the time an object is carried should be included in the time the object is lifted since one must also lift while carrying. Carrying time should never exceed lifting time. "Here is a guiding example: If a worker is required to stand at a bench and lift 25-pound objects for a total of 2 hours, and is also required to carry the 25-pound objects away from the bench for a total of 1 hour, then the analyst should record that the job requires lifting 25 pounds for 3 hours and carrying 25 pounds for 1 hour."[12]

The factors of lifting and carrying are broken down into 12 sub-factors, representing different weights.

Pushing (1-12) "Exerting muscular force upon an object so that the force is directed away from the person, including slapping and striking."

Pulling (1-12) "Exerting muscular force upon an object so that the force is directed toward the person, including jerking.

"The factors of Pushing and Pulling are most complex. . . . It may be thought that pushing or pulling with a 20-pound force requires little effort and that pushing or pulling with a 200-pound force requires great effort, while, depending upon the body position, the exact opposite may be true.

[10] *Ibid.*, p. 103. For a helpful discussion of time requirements see pp. 103-106.
[11] *Ibid.*, p. 128.
[12] *Loc. cit.*

"Because of this complication, it is better that the analyst convert the pushing or pulling force required into its *equivalent of lifting* so many pounds, that is, when pushing or pulling are required from stationary positions such as Sitting, Standing, Stooping, and Reclining. When, however, pushing and pulling are required while moving, as in pushing a hand truck, then the force exerted should be converted into its *equivalent of carrying* so many pounds (remembering that carrying also includes lifting).

"Unfortunately . . . there is no conversion table to assist the analyst in calculating the lifting and carrying equivalents of pushing and pulling efforts. But, even so, the analyst's guess as to the lifting or carrying equivalent is better than showing the actual force exerted in pushing and pulling when registered on a scale.

"As an example of estimating pushing and pulling effort in terms of lifting and carrying equivalents, a truck driver, when turning the wheels of a parked truck, may pull on the steering wheel with a force of around 100 pounds if registered on a scale. This pulling effort, however, would probably not be greater than lifting 25 pounds. The analyst, then, would record the length of time this effort is required and indicate it under lifting 25 pounds."[13]

Fingering (13-14) "Picking, pinching, or otherwise working with dexterous movements of the fingers of either or both hands. Not to be confused with handling.

Handling (15-16) "Seizing, holding, grasping, turning, or otherwise working with the hands of either or both arms. Not to be confused with the dexterous movements of fingering.

Reaching (17-20) "Extending the hands and arms in any direction, reaching above or below shoulder height with either or both arms.

Throwing (21-22) "Propelling an object through space by a swinging motion of either or both hands and arms either with or without the use of tongs or other devices.

Sitting (23) "Resting upon the haunches as in occupying a bench, chair, or saddle. Squatting, sitting on the heels, or sitting on the ground, should be considered as crouching, not as sitting.

Total time on feet (24) "This period is the maximum number of hours the job requires the worker to be on his feet during the

[13] *Ibid.,* pp. 130-131.

work shift. For the usual routine job, total time on feet should equal the sum of the time required by the separate factors of standing, walking, climbing, jumping, and running.

Standing (25) "Supporting oneself on either or both feet and legs in an upright or nearly upright position.

*   *   *   *

Climbing—legs only (29) "Ascending or descending such fixtures or places as ramps, stairs, and hills by using the legs and feet only.

Climbing—legs and arms (30) "Ascending or descending such fixtures as ladders, scaffoldings, poles, and ropes by using the hands and arms in addition to the feet and legs.

Treading (31-34) "Exerting force upon an object with either or both feet and legs. This activity may be required while sitting, as in operating the pedals of an automobile, or while standing, as in operating a clothes press.

Stooping (35) "Bending the body downward from a standing position by bending the spine at the waist, including the act of remaining in this position. Not to be confused with crouching.

Crouching (36) "Bending the body downward from a standing position by bending the legs in addition to bending the spine, including squatting, sitting on the heels, and sitting on the ground; also including the acts of remaining in these positions. Not to be confused with stooping.

"Stooping and crouching from the stationary position of standing should not be considered as distinct from standing. The time the worker is required to stoop or crouch should be included in the time the worker is required to stand. Should the worker stoop or crouch while walking or running, the time should be included in the time for walking or running.

Kneeling (37) "Bending the legs at the knees to come to rest on the knee or knees, including the act of remaining on the knee or knees.

Crawling (38) "Moving about on the hands and knees or hands and feet.

Reclining (39) "Assuming a horizontal working position on the back, belly or side.

Twisting (40) "Turning the body partly around from stationary positions such as standing, sitting, kneeling and reclining, involving a tension on the body muscles and spine, and including the acts of remaining in these positions. Stooping backward should be considered as twisting, not as stooping.

Waiting time (41) "Inaction due to the intermittent nature of the job, as in the case of a tack welder who is required to be inactive while waiting for other workers to prepare the materials to be welded.

"If a job requires the worker to have periods of inaction totaling 2 hours per day, the analyst should show these 2 hours under waiting time and not under sitting, standing, or walking even though the worker may sit, stand or walk during these 2 hours. Periods of inaction should be treated in this manner due to the usually optional nature of body positions and activities during such periods.

Seeing (42-45) "Perceiving the nature of objects by sight.

"Although it is not difficult for physicians to determine the visual acuity of workers, there is no accurate method for determining the visual requirements of jobs because of an almost endless chain of variables which makes the actual job situation differ from the laboratory environment in which visual standards are established. Surprising though it may be, even industrial ophthalmologists only guess at what jobs require visually. And still other professional people have confused the issue profoundly by mistakenly claiming that the vision possessed by the best workers on any job is the vision required by that job."[14]

Tables are available to guide the analyst in estimating the far and near visual requirements of jobs. The tables show the visual acuities required to see these objects at various distances.

Far Vision (42) "In estimating job requirements for far vision, the analyst should determine the size of the smallest, most difficult object the job requires the worker to see at a distance of 5 feet or more, and also the distance the worker is required to be from the object."[15]

After establishing the size and distance of the object, the analyst can then refer to the visual acuity table that has been prescribed for his use.

Near vision (43) "Here the analyst determines the size of the smallest, most difficult object the worker is required to see at a close working distance of about 14 inches, such as ruler graduations of 1/32 of an inch."[16]

---

[14] *Ibid.*, pp. 131-134.
[15] *Ibid.*, p. 135.
[16] *Ibid.*, p. 138.

After establishing the size and distance of the object, the analyst can then refer to the *near* visual acuity table that has been prescribed for his use.

Color Vision (44) "Perceiving the color of objects by sight.

Depth Perception (45) "Perceiving distances of an object from the observer or from one object to another at different distances from the observer. This factor usually is required by most jobs involving machine operations and mobile equipment.

Hearing (46) "Perceiving the nature of sound by ear.

Talking (47) "Expressing ideas by means of the spoken word.

Other (48-49) "Write-in space for any other physical factors the job analyst may encounter. . . .

Definitions of the Environmental Factors

Inside (50) "Indoor protection from weather conditions.

Outside—Fair weather (51) "Out of doors or under an overhead covering with slight protection from the weather during stormless periods.

Outside—Wet weather (52) "Out of doors or under an overhead covering with slight protection from the weather during stormless periods.

Hot (53) "Temperature sufficiently high to cause perceptible bodily discomfort usually found on jobs which require work around furnaces or fire.

Cold (54) "Temperature sufficiently low to cause perceptible bodily discomfort usually found on jobs which require work in refrigerated rooms.

Sudden Temperature Changes (55) "Variations in temperature which are sufficiently marked and abrupt to cause perceptible bodily reactions. Jobs which involve excessive heat or cold also invariably involve sudden temperature changes.

Humid (56) "Atmospheric conditions with moisture content sufficiently high to cause perceptible bodily discomfort.

Dry (57) "Atmospheric conditions with moisture content sufficiently low to cause perceptible bodily discomfort.

"Hot, Cold, Sudden Temperature Changes, Humid, and Dry are to be considered by the analyst only when these factors are caused by conditions other than the weather itself. This is done because the weather conditions for a locality are usually a matter of common knowledge and hence no need exists for recording the seasonal temperatures for each job. An exception may be when an indoor job is performed in an unheated building in a locality where the winters are severe, or in a poorly ventilated building, where the summers are excessively warm. In such cases, the analyst should add a W or an S after the degrees of temperature recorded for cold or hot to show that the excessive temperatures exist only in winter or summer.

Moving Objects (58) "Exposure to moving equipment and objects such as overhead cranes, hand and motor driven vehicles, and falling objects which involves the risk of bodily injury; also the act of operating such equipment, as in driving a truck.

Hazardous Machinery (59) "Exposure to the moving parts of stationary machinery which involves the risk of bodily injury.

Sharp Tools or Materials (60) "Exposure to tools and materials with sharp edges which involves the risk of bodily injury.

Cluttered Floors (61) "Walking surface of workplace necessarily strewn with equipment, tools, or materials (not a condition of poor housekeeping), which involves the risk of bodily injury through tripping and falling.

Slippery Floors (62) "Walking surface of workplace which involves the risk of slipping and falling due to such agents as grease, oil, water, and polish, or due to wear as in the case of steel surfaces.

High Places (63) "Workplace at an elevation above the floor or ground level from which it is possible to fall and be injured.

Electrical Hazards (64) "Exposure to electric wires, transformers, bus bars, or other uninsulated or unshielded electrical parts or equipment which involves the risk of bodily injury, or general or fatal electric shock.

Exposure to burns (65) "Workplace which involves the risk of burns from hot materials, fire or chemical agents.

Explosives (66) "Exposure to explosive gases, vapors, dusts, liquids, and substances which involves the risk of general or fatal injury.

Radiant Energy (67) "Exposure to: (a) radio-active substances such as radium, uranium, or thorium; (b) to X-Rays; or (c) to ultra-violet or infrared rays which involves the risk of impairment of sight or general or localized disabling conditions.

"The analyst is to state the kind of radiation encountered on the job. If numerous kinds are found in a plant, it becomes necessary to make up a system for coding the various kinds found for presentation in the master chart under the one heading of radiant energy.

Poor Lighting (68) "Illumination of workplace below the standards set by the American Standards Association Code.

Poor Ventilation (69) "Air condition of workplace below the standards set by the American Standards Association Code.

Toxic Conditions (70) "Exposure to harmful fumes, gases, vapors, mists, liquids, dusts, greases, or solids which may cause general or localized disabling conditions as a result of inhalation, ingestion, or absorption by the skin.

"The analyst is to state the kind of toxic conditions found on the job. If numerous kinds are found in a plant, it becomes necessary to make up a system for coding the various kinds found for presentation in the master chart under the one heading of toxic conditions.

Wet Quarters (71) "Workplace requiring contact with water or other liquid.

Close Quarters (72) "Workplace where freedom of movement is restricted or where the worker must maintain a stooped or cramped position.

Vibration (73) "Production of a quivering movement of the body muscles, particularly those of the legs and arms, as from repeated motion, pressure, or shock.

Noise (74) "(a) Sufficient sound to distract workers engaged in 'mental' occupations, such as sounds greater than those made by typewriters or other common office equipment. (b) Sufficient sound to cause possible injury to the sense of hearing of workers engaged in 'manual' occupations, such as sounds from nearby chipping and riveting operations in a shipyard.

Working with Others (75) "Job requiring direct occupational cooperation with fellow workers or direct contact with the public.

Working Around Others (76) "Job requiring independent occupational effort but in proximity to fellow workers or the public.

Working Alone (77) "Job requiring independent occupational effort and virtually no contact with fellow workers or the public.

Shifts (78) "The work periods established by the plant for the job being analyzed. . . .

Other (79-80) "Write-in space for any other environmental factors the analyst may encounter in rare instances. . . ."[17]

[17] *Ibid.*, pp. 139-143.

APPENDIX III

Circular Letters of Company Officers on Placing Partially Disabled Employees

ALUMINUM COMPANY OF CANADA, LIMITED
ARVIDA WORKS

22 November 1954

CIRCULAR LETTER

This is to acquaint you with our program to improve placement procedures for employees who become partially disabled because of accidents, sickness or aging. The program is intended to give us better answers to the question: For what jobs is the handicapped employee physically qualified?

The program includes:

1. — Surveying the Works to find 70 to 80 jobs which may be suitable for persons with some kind of disability. Jobs are being selected which differ considerably in the degree of skill needed.

2. — Analyzing the physical and environmental requirements of those jobs.

3. — Giving medical examinations to employees in such a way that their physical and environmental capacities can be compared with particular job requirements. This will make it possible to deal positively with the abilities of employees who have some physical impairment, rather than with their disabilities.

4. — Predicting the extent of future placement needs.

5. — Planning to meet future placement needs.

The program is being carried through by Messrs. Alex. Morin and L. G. Mousseau of the Personnel Division, and Dr. Elmer

159

Luchterhand, Staff Training and Research Division, Montreal. Messrs. Fortunat Lafrance, Jacques Mailly and Jules Pilote, all safety inspectors, will assist in the preliminary survey and in analyzing physical and environmental requirements.

It is important to note practices and procedures with which the program is *not* concerned:

1. — It will not alter the generally desirable practice of attempting to place handicapped employees within their own departments and sections.

2. — It is not concerned with wage determinations.

3. — Since the program deals with the problem of placing the handicapped, it is not concerned with increasing work loads.

In analyzing physical and environmental demands, it will be necessary to ask supervisory personnel for their judgements and for the verification of the analyses. We would appreciate it if you would acquaint your supervisory personnel, including general foremen, with this program.

JJG:RP   J. J. GAGNON
                                    Personnel Manager,
                                    Arvida Works

ALUMINUM COMPANY OF CANADA, LIMITED

Telephone: University 6-7511   MONTREAL
Cable: Alcan Montreal   1700 Sun Life Building

10 January 1958

CIRCULAR LETTER

Subject: The Arvida Placement System

Under separate cover, we are sending you a copy of Part 1 of the *Arvida Placement System*. This report reviews initial operation of the Arvida Placement System from June 1955 to December 1956. While this report has been available on request previously, we are now making a formal distribution to insure greater familiarity with it.

It may be of interest to mention the reception given this report by others. The January 1958 issue of *Aging*, a monthly publication of the United States Department of Health, Education and Welfare, includes a review which states:

"This is a 14-page report of a highly imaginative and successful procedure to place handicapped as well as older workers in selected jobs which are suited to their capacities and the demands of which do not conflict with specific disabilities or loss of energy due to old age. The plan, which is in operation in a large manufacturing concern, involves detailed analysis of each job, physical assessment of each worker in relation to job requirements, and full understanding and co-operation on the part of workers, supervisors, industrial physicians, and management. The report states that 'in a strict sense, (there are) no handicapped people.' The system is now standard procedure in the Arvida Works of the Aluminum Company of Canada, Limited."

A letter from the same United States government department requesting copies of the report for distribution to their state and territorial rehabilitation agencies states:

"We plan to bring your project results to their attention. Your findings, we believe, will have implications also for the field of placement for the handicapped generally in this country."

Besides these indications of interest, it has been reported that favourable reference to the Arvida Placement System was made at the recent American Manufacturers' Association meeting in New York. Much interest has also been shown in a recent meeting of Alcan physicians, called by Dr. F. D. Brent.

It is our feeling that this report should be given wide distribution throughout the Company as other Alcan plants, besides Arvida, might profit by studying and possibly developing somewhat similar systems. In the event that you would contemplate the organization of a local committee, we are able to provide you with some help. To assist such efforts, we would be glad to make available the services of Dr. Elmer Luchterhand, for temporary assignment at plants. Dr. Luchterhand, whose field is social research, was directly responsible to Arvida Works for the developmental and initial organizational work on the placement system. It may be mentioned that at Arvida, all work was done by special assignment of interested people.

RN:JAB

> RODNEY NORTHEY
> Vice President and
> Director of Personnel

Selected Bibliography

Many hundreds of meritorious research works relevant to accident and illness problems, aging, blue-collar life, and placement procedures and choice, might have been listed under the headings of this bibliography. The items included were selected for the light they throw on the problems treated in this study.

I
BLUE-COLLAR WORLDS

ANDERSON, NELS. *Dimensions of Work: The Sociology of a Work Culture.* New York: David McKay Company, Inc., 1964.

ARGYRIS, CHRIS. "The Individual and Organization: Some Problems of Mutual Adjustment," *Administrative Science Quarterly,* Vol. 2 (1957), pp. 1-24.

BAKKE, E. WIGHT. *The Unemployed Worker.* New Haven: Yale University Press, 1940.

BLAUNER, ROBERT. *Alienation and Freedom: The Factory Worker and His Industry.* Chicago: The University of Chicago Press, 1964.

DEAN, DWIGHT G. "Alienation: Its Meaning and Measurement," *American Sociological Review,* Vol. 26 (1961), pp. 753-758.

DUBIN, ROBERT. "Industrial Workers' Worlds," *Social Problems,* Vol. 3, No. 3 (January 1956), pp. 131-142.

FAUNCE, WILLIAM A. "Automation and the Division of Labor," *Social Problems,* Vol. 13, No. 2 (Fall 1965), pp. 149-160.

FEUER, LEWIS. "What is Alienation? The Career of a Concept," *New Politics,* Vol. 1, No. 3 (Spring 1962), pp. 116-134.

FRIEDMANN, GEORGE. *The Anatomy of Work.* New York: The Free Press of Glencoe, Inc., 1961.

FROMM, ERICH. *The Sane Society.* New York: Rinehart, 1955.

GLAZER, NATHAN. "The Alienation of Modern Man," *Commentary,* Vol. 4 (1947), p. 380.

GOODMAN, PAUL. *Growing Up Absurd.* New York: Random House, 1960.

HAMMOND, GUYTON B. *Man in Estrangement.* Nashville: Vanderbilt University Press, 1965.

H.R.H. The Duke of Edinburgh's Study Conference, 1956. *Background Papers,* Vol. II. London: Oxford University Press, 1957. In particular: ELMER LUCHTERHAND, "Social Planning and Adjustment at Kitimat."

Institute of Local Government. *Single-Enterprise Communities in Canada.* Kingston, Ontario: Queen's University, 1953. (Photo offset.)

JASPERS, KARL. *Man in the Modern Age.* Garden City, New York: Doubleday Anchor Books, 1957.

MILLER, S. M., and FRANK RIESSMAN. "The Working Class Subculture: A New View," *Social Problems,* Vol. 9, No. 1 (1961), pp. 86-97.

MILLS, C. WRIGHT (ed). *Images of Man.* New York: George Braziller, Inc., 1960. See especially the chapter on alienation containing the writings of Karl Marx and Friedrich Engels, pp. 486-507.

MORSE, NANCY C., and R. S. WEISS. "The Function and Meaning of Work and the Job," *American Sociological Review,* Vol. 20 (April 1955), pp. 191-198.

NEAL, ARTHUR G., and S. RETTIG. "Dimensions of Alienation among Manual and Non-manual Workers," *American Sociological Review,* Vol. 28 (1963), pp. 599-608.

NISBET, ROBERT. *The Quest for Community.* New York: Oxford University Press, 1953.

PAPPENHEIM, FRITZ. *The Alienation of Modern Man.* New York: Monthly Review Press, 1959.

SCOTT, THOMAS B., *et al. A Theory of Work Adjustment.* Minneapolis, Minnesota: Industrial Relations Center, University of Minnesota, 1964.

SEEMAN, MELVIN. "On the Meaning of Alienation," *American Sociological Review,* Vol. 24 (1959), pp. 783-791.

SHOSTAK, ARTHUR B., and WILLIAM GOMBERG (eds.) *Blue-Collar World: Studies of the American Worker.* Englewood Cliffs, New Jersey: Prentice-Hall, Inc., 1964.

SWADOS, HARVEY. "The Myth of the Happy Worker," in ERIC and MARY JOSEPHSON (eds.), *Man Alone.* New York: Dell Publishing Company, Inc., 1962.

SYKES, GERALD (ed.). *Alienation: The Cultural Climate of our Time.* New York: George Braziller, 1964.

WARNER, W. L., and J. O. Low. *The Social System of the Modern Factory.* New Haven: Yale University Press. 1947.

II

ACCIDENTS, ILLNESS AND WORK

ALLAN, W. SCOTT. *Rehabilitation: A Community Challenge.* New York: John Wiley & Sons, Inc., 1958.

BARKER, R. G. "The Social Psychology of Physical Disability," *Journal of Social Issues,* Vol. 4 (1948).

BARKER, R. G., B. A. WRIGHT, L. MEYERSON and M. R. GONICK. *Adjustment to Physical Handicap and Illness: A Survey of the Social Psychology of Physique and Disability,* Bull. No. 55, revised. New York: Social Science Research Council, 1953.

CHEIT, E. F. *Injury and Recovery in the Course of Employment.* New York: John Wiley, 1961.

DAVIS, FRED. *Passage Through Crisis.* Indianapolis: The Bobbs-Merrill Co., 1963.

————. "Deviance Disavowal: The Management of Strained Interaction by the Visibly Handicapped," in HOWARD S. BECKER, *The Other Side, Perspectives on Deviance.* New York: Free Press of Glencoe, 1964. Pp. 119-137.

DEMBO, T., G. L. LEVITON and B. A. WRIGHT. "Adjustment to Misfortune: A Problem of Social-Psychological Rehabilitation," *Artificial Limbs,* Vol. 3, No. 2 (Autumn 1956), pp. 4-62.

FISHMAN, SIDNEY. *Self-Concepts and Adjustment to Leg Prosthesis.* New York: Columbia University, 1949.

————. "Amputee Needs, Frustrations, and Behavior," *Rehabilitation Literature,* Vol. 20, No. 11 (November 1959), pp. 322-329.

FREIDSON, ELIOT. "Disability as Social Deviance," in MARVIN B. SUSSMAN (ed.), *Sociology and Rehabilitation.* Washington, D.C.: American Sociological Association, 1966.

GARFINKEL, H. "Conditions of Successful Degradation Ceremonies," *American Journal of Sociology,* Vol. 61 (1956), pp. 420-424.

GELLMAN, W. "Roots of Prejudice Against the Handicapped,"

Journal of Rehabilitation, Vol. 25, No. 1 (January-February 1959), pp. 4-6.

HABER, W. B. "Effects of Loss of Limb on Sensory Functions," *Journal of Psychology*, Vol. 40 (1955), pp. 115-123.

HEWES, AMY. "Study of Accident Records in a Textile Mill," *Journal of Industrial Hygiene*, Vol. 3, No. 6 (1921-22), pp. 187-195.

JACO, E. GARTLEY (ed.). *Patients, Physicians and Illness.* Glencoe, Illinois: The Free Press, 1958.

KESSLER, HENRY H. *Rehabilitation of the Physically Handicapped.* 2nd ed. New York: Columbia University Press, 1958.

KING, STANLEY H. *Perceptions of Illness and Medical Practice.* New York: Russell Sage Foundation, 1962.

KRUSEN, F. H. *Concepts in Rehabilitation of the Handicapped.* Philadelphia: W. B. Saunders, 1964.

LADIEU, G., E. HAUFMANN and T. DEMBO. "Studies in Adjustment to Visible Injuries," *Journal of Abnormal and Social Psychology*, Vol. 42 (1947), pp. 169-192.

LINDUSKA, L. *My Polio Past.* Chicago: Pellegrini and Cudahy, 1947.

LIVINGSTON, S. *Living with Epileptic Seizures.* Springfield: Charles C. Thomas, 1963.

McGOWAN, JOHN F. (ed.). *An Introduction to the Vocational Rehabilitation Process.* Washington, D.C.: U.S. Vocational Rehabilitation Administration, 1960.

MEYERSON, L. "Physical Disability as a Social Psychological Problem," *Journal of Social Issues*, Vol. 4, No. 4 (1948), pp. 2-10.

————. "Experimental Injury: An Approach to the Dynamics of Physical Disability," *Journal of Social Issues*, Vol. 4 (1948), pp. 68-71.

MYERS, JEROME K. "Consequences and Prognoses of Disability," in MARVIN B. SUSSMAN (ed.), *Sociology and Rehabilitation.* Washington, D.C.: American Sociological Association, 1966.

NAGRI, SAAD Z. "Some Conceptual Issues in Disability and Rehabilitation," in MARVIN B. SUSSMAN (ed.), *Sociology and Rehabilitation.* Washington, D.C.: American Sociological Association, 1966.

RIESSMAN, FRANK, JEROME COHEN and ARTHUR PEARL (eds.). *Mental Health of the Poor.* New York: The Free Press of Glencoe, 1964.

ROTH, JULIUS. *Timetables*. Indianapolis: The Bobbs-Merrill Co., Inc., 1963.

RUSSELL, H. *Victory in My Hands*. New York: Creative Age Press, 1949.

SPENCER, W. A. "Expanded Horizons and Problems in the Management of Disability," *Journal of American Physical Therapy Association*, Vol. 44, No. 11 (1964), pp. 978-985.

STRAUS, ROBERT. "Social Change and the Rehabilitation Concept," in MARVIN B. SUSSMAN (ed.), *Sociology and Rehabilitation*. Washington, D.C.: American Sociological Association, 1966.

SUCHMAN, EDWARD A. "A Model for Research and Evaluation on Rehabilitation," in MARVIN B. SUSSMAN (ed.), *Sociology and Rehabilitation*. Washington, D.C.: American Sociological Association, 1966.

SUSSMANN, MARVIN B. "Occupational Sociology and Rehabilitation," in MARVIN B. SUSSMAN (ed.), *Sociology and Rehabilitation*. Washington, D.C.: American Sociological Association, 1966.

TOYNBEE, P. (ed.). *Underdogs*. London: Weidenfeld and Nicolson, 1961.

WHITE, R. K., B. A. WRIGHT and T. DEMBO. "Studies in Adjustment to Visible Injuries: Evaluation of Curiosity by the Insured," *Journal of Abnormal and Social Psychology*, Vol. 43 (1948), pp. 13-28.

WRIGHT, BEATRICE A. *Physical Disability, A Psychological Approach*. New York: Harper & Row, 1960.

III

AGING AND WORK

BELBIN, DR. R. M. *Training Methods for Older Workers*. Paris: Organisation for Economic Co-Operation and Development, 1965.

BOTWINICK, J., and N. W. SHOCK. "Age Changes in Performance Decrement with Continuous Work," *Journal of Gerontology*, Vol. 7, No. 1 (1952), pp. 41-46.

BRECKENRIDGE, ELIZABETH. *Effective Use of Older Workers*, Chicago: Wilcox & Follet Co., 1953.

CLARK, F. LeGROS. "Physical Problems in the Employment of Aging Men," *International Labour Review*, Vol. 76 (1957), pp. 367-83.

168 CHOICE IN HUMAN AFFAIRS

Cumming, Elaine, and William E. Henry. *Growing Old.* New York: Basic Books, Inc., 1961.

Donahue, Wilma, James Rae, Jr., and Roger B. Berry. *Rehabilitation of Older Workers.* Ann Arbor, Michigan: University of Michigan Press, 1953.

Douse, H. L. "Discrimination Against Older Workers," *International Labour Review*, Vol. 83 (April 1961), pp. 349-68.

Friedman, E. A., and R. J. Havighurst, *et al. The Meaning of Work and Retirement.* Chicago: University of Chicago Press, 1954.

Gordon, Margaret S. "The Older Worker and Hiring Practices," *Monthly Labor Review*, Vol. 82, (November 1959), pp. 1198-1205.

Granick, Samuel. "Studies in the Psychology of Senility—A survey," *Journal of Gerontology*, Vol. 5, No. 1 (1950), pp. 44-58.

Hauser, Phillip M. "Changes in the Labor-force Participation of the Older Worker," *American Journal of Sociology*, Vol. 59, No. 4 (1954), pp. 312-323.

International Labour Organization. "The Aging Worker in the Canadian Economy: Recent Studies on Employment Problems of Older Workers," *Industry and Labour*, Vol. 23 (1960), pp. 353-372.

McFarland, R. A. "The Older Workers in Industry," *The Harvard Business Review*, Vol. 21, No. 4 (1943), pp. 505-520.

Murrell, K. F. H. "Major Problems of Industrial Gerontology," *Journal of Gerontology*, Vol. 14 (April 1959), pp. 216-221.

Sheppard, Harold L., Louis A. Ferman and Seymour Faber. *Too Old to Work—Too Young to Retire: A Case Study of a Permanent Plant Shutdown.* Washington, D.C.: Government Printing Office, 1960.

Switzer, Mary E., and Howard A. Rusk. "Keeping Older People Fit for Participation," *The Annals of the American Academy of Political and Social Science*, Vol. 279 (January 1952), pp. 146-154.

Tibbitts, Clark, and Wilma Donahue (eds.). *Aging in Today's Society.* Englewood Cliffs, New Jersey: Prentice-Hall, 1960.

United Kingdom Ministry of Labour. "Employment of Older Men and Women," *Labour Gazette* (Canada), Vol. 57, (September 1957), pp. 1054-1057.

IV

PLACEMENT: PROBLEMS, PROCEDURES AND EVALUATION

BRAMBLETT, EARL R. "Problems of Management in the Placement of Handicapped Workers," *Archives of Physical Medicine and Rehabilitation*, Vol. 37, No. 9 (September 1956), pp. 547-549.

BRIDGES, CLARK D. *Job Placement of the Physically Handicapped*. New York: McGraw-Hill Book Company, Inc., 1946.

EGGERS, E. T. "Employment of the Physically Handicapped," *Industrial Medicine and Surgery*, Vol. 29, (September 1960), pp. 427-433.

GOFFMAN, ERVING. *Stigma: Notes on the Management of Spoiled Identity*. Englewood Cliffs, New Jersey: Prentice-Hall, Inc., 1963.

GRIEW, STEPHEN. *Job Re-Design*. Paris: Organisation for Economic Co-Operation and Development, 1964.

HANMAN, BERT. *Physical Capacities and Job Placement*. Stockholm: Nordisk Rotogravyr, 1951.

HIRSCH, DORIS K. "A Work Trial Program for the Severely Handicapped," *Journal of Rehabilitation*, Vol. 16, No. 6 (November-December 1950), pp. 3-6.

IRVIN, E. A. "Industrial Placement of the Physically Handicapped," *Archives of Physical Medicine and Rehabilitation*, Vol. 37, No. 10 (October 1956), pp. 622-626.

KELLOGG, WILLIAM A. *Pre-Employment Disability Evaluation*. Springfield, Illinois: Charles C. Thomas, 1957.

National Industrial Conference Board. *The Company and the Physically Impaired Worker*. Studies in Personnel Policy, No. 163, 1957.

ODELL, CHARLES E. "Employment Services for Older Workers," *The Annals of the American Academy of Political and Social Science*, Vol. 279 (January 1952), pp. 171-179.

Physical Abilities to Fit the Job. Boston: American Mutual Liability Insurance Company, 1956.

SCOTT, THOMAS B., *et al*. *A Follow-Up Study of Placement Success*. Minneapolis, Minnesota: Industrial Relations Center, University of Minnesota, 1958.

————. *A Study of 1,637 DVR Counselees*. Minneapolis,

Minnesota: Industrial Relations Center, University of Minnesota, 1958.

————. *Factors Related to Employment Success.* Minneapolis, Minnesota: Industrial Relations Center, University of Minnesota, 1959.

————. *A Study of Employment Service Applicants.* Minneapolis, Minnesota: Industrial Relations Center, University of Minnesota, 1960.

————. *The Application of Research Results.* Minneapolis, Minnesota: Industrial Relations Center, University of Minnesota, 1960.

————. *A Definition of Work Adjustment.* Minneapolis, Minnesota: Industrial Relations Center, University of Minnesota, 1960.

————. *Attitudinal Barriers to Employment.* Minneapolis, Minnesota: Industrial Relations Center, University of Minnesota, 1961.

————. *The Measurement of Vocational Needs.* Minneapolis, Minnesota: Industrial Relations Center, University of Minnesota, 1964.

VINEBERG, S. E. "Concerning Job Readiness," *Journal of Rehabilitation,* Vol. 24, No. 6 (November-December 1958), pp. 9-10.

SOBEL, IRVIN, and RICHARD C. WILCOCK. *Placement Techniques for Older Workers.* Paris: Organisation for Economic Cooperation and Development, 1966.

VISCARDI, HENRY, JR. *Give Us the Tools.* New York: Eriksson-Taplinger Co., 1959.

V

CHOICE AND DECISIONS: THEORY AND RESEARCH

ARGYRIS, CHRIS. *Organization and Innovation.* Homewood, Ill.: Richard D. Irwin, Inc., and The Dorsey Press, 1965.

ADAMS, J. S., and W. B. ROSENBAUM. "The Relationship of Worker Productivity to Cognitive Dissonance," *Journal of Applied Psychology,* Vol. 46 (1962), pp. 161-164.

ATKINSON, J. W. "Motivational Determinants of Risk-taking Behavior," *Psychological Review,* Vol. 64 (1957), pp. 359-372.

BERKOWITZ, L. "The Judgmental Process in Personality Functioning," *Psychological Review,* Vol. 67 (1960), pp. 130-142.

BREHM, J. W. "Post-decision Changes in the Desirability of Alternatives," *Journal of Abnormal and Social Psychology,* Vol. 52 (1956), pp. 384-389.

————. "Increasing Cognitive Dissonance by a Fait-accompli," *Journal of Abnormal and Social Psychology,* Vol. 58 (1959), pp. 379-382.

————. "Attitudinal Consequences of Commitment to Unpleasant Behavior," *Journal of Abnormal and Social Psychology,* Vol. 60 (1960), pp. 379-383.

————. "Motivational Effects of Cognitive Dissonance," in M. R. JONES (ed.), *Nebraska Symposium on Motivation.* Lincoln: University of Nebraska Press, 1962.

BREHM, J. W., and A. R. COHEN. "Choice and Chance Relative Deprivation as Determinants of Cognitive Dissonance," *Journal of Abnormal and Social Psychology,* Vol. 58 (1959), pp. 383-387.

————. *Explorations in Cognitive Dissonance.* New York: John Wiley & Sons, 1962.

BROCK, T. C. "Cognitive Restructuring and Attitude Change," *Journal of Abnormal and Social Psychology,* Vol. 64 (1962), pp. 264-271.

BROWN, J. "Principles of Intrapersonal Conflict." *Journal of Conflict Resolution,* Vol. 1 (1957), pp. 135-154.

BRUNER, J. S., and H. TAJFEL. "Cognitive Risk and Environmental Changes," *Journal of Abnormal and Social Psychology,* Vol. 62 (1961), pp. 231-234.

COHEN, A. R. *Attitude Change and Social Influence.* New York: Basic Books, 1964.

COHEN, A. R., J. W. BREHM and W. H. FLEMING. "Attitude Change and Justification for Compliance," *Journal of Abnormal and Social Psychology,* Vol. 56 (1958), pp. 276-278.

COHEN, A. R., H. I. TERRY and C. B. JONES. "Attitudinal Effects of Choice in Exposure to Counter-Propaganda," *Journal of Abnormal and Social Psychology,* Vol. 58 (1959), pp. 388-391.

DAVIDOFF, PAUL, and THOMAS A. REINER. "A Choice Theory of Planning," *Journal of the American Institute of Planners,* Vol. 28 (May, 1962), pp. 103-115.

EDWARDS, T. "The Theory of Decision-Making," *Psychological Bulletin,* Vol. 51 (1954), pp. 380-417.

FESTINGER, LEON. *A Theory of Cognitive Dissonance*. New York: Harper & Row, 1957.

————. *Conflict, Decision and Dissonance*, Stanford, California: Stanford University Press, 1964.

FESTINGER, L., and J. M. CARLSMITH. "Cognitive Consequences of Forced Compliance," *Journal of Abnormal and Social Psychology*, Vol. 58 (1959), pp. 203-210.

JANIS, I. L. "Decisional Conflicts: A Theoretical Analysis," *Journal of Conflict Resolution*, Vol. 3 (1959), pp. 6-27.

————. "Motivational Factors in the Resolution of Decisional Conflicts," in M. R. JONES (ed.), *Nebraska Symposium on Motivation*. Lincoln: University of Nebraska Press, 1959.

KOGAN, NATHAN, and MICHAEL A. WALLACH. *Risk Taking: A Study in Cognition and Personality*. New York: Holt, Rinehart and Winston, 1964.

LUCHTERHAND, ELMER. "Research and the Dilemmas in Developing Social Programs," in P. LAZARSFELD, W. SEWELL and H. WILENSKY (eds.), *The Uses of Sociology*. New York: Basic Books, in press.

MACHOL, ROBERT E. (ed.). *Information and Decision Processes*. New York: McGraw-Hill, 1960.

RESTLE, F. *Psychology of Judgement and Choice*. New York: John Wiley & Sons, 1961.

SMITH, E. E. "The Power of Dissonance Techniques to Change Attitudes," *Public Opinion Quarterly*, Vol. 25 (1961), pp. 626-639.

TAYLOR, D. W. (ed.). *Experiments on Decision-making and Other Studies*. Arlington, Va.: ASTIA (Technical Report No. 6, AD 253952), pp. 1-11.

WALLACH, M. A., and N. KOGAN. "Aspects of Judgment and Decision-making: Interrelationships and Changes with Age," *Behavioral Science*, Vol. 6 (1961), pp. 23-36.

Index

173